The National P[...]
Shaping the System

Produced by
Harpers Ferry Center
National Park Service

U.S. Department of the Interior
Washington, D.C.

From the Director

The Statue of Liberty, Yellowstone, Everglades, Grand Canyon, Independence Hall, Carlsbad Caverns—these names are known to school children and adults throughout the United States and around the world. The places these names represent are only a few of the 388 natural, cultural, and recreational areas that make up the National Park System. This collection of special places welcomes upwards of 280 million visitors every year who come to learn, enjoy, and be awed and inspired. Congress has described the System, which includes some of the most significant historic and natural places in the nation, as "cumulative expressions of a single national heritage." These national parks form the backbone of a nationwide system of local, county, state, and regional parks that provides recreational and educational opportunities for everyone.

The story of the creation of this amazing system of parks is the subject of this book. It begins in 1832 in Hot Springs, Arkansas, and threads its way through the Yosemite Valley, across the bloodied fields at Gettysburg and Shiloh, along the spine of the Appalachian Mountains, and down to seashores along the Pacific and Atlantic coasts and the Gulf of Mexico. It speaks to a determined and prolonged effort to set aside and preserve some of the best places this country possesses. It is my honor to serve as the 16th Director of the National Park Service as we protect and preserve this national legacy. It is also my great pleasure to present this story to you. I hope it will inspire and inform and spark your interest in participating in the richness of the National Park System. As always, I'll see you in the parks!

Fran P. Mainella, Director
National Park Service

Red mangrove trees seem to float on water at Everglades National Park in Florida.

Using this Book

This book tells the story of the evolution of the U.S. National Park System, the first of its kind in the world. In Part 1 former Bureau Historian Barry Mackintosh discusses the origins of the System and describes the complexity of its designations. In Part 2 Mackintosh chronicles the step-by-step growth of the System from its beginnings to its 388 areas at the beginning of 2005. Part 3 contains maps showing the extent of the System and its growth over time, a list of all National Park Service directors with their tenures, a feature on individuals who helped make the System what it is today, and suggested readings. An index completes the book.

This is the third print edition of *The National Parks: Shaping the System*, which was first published in 1985. The text has been updated by Bureau Historian Janet McDonnell.

National Park Handbooks support management programs and promote understanding and enjoyment of the more than 380 parks in the National Park System. The National Park Service cares for these special places saved by the American people so that all may enjoy our heritage. Handbooks are sold at parks and can be purchased by mail from: U.S. Government Printing Office, Stop SSOP, Washington, DC 20402-0001 or online at bookstore.gpo.gov.

Library of Congress Cataloging-in-Publication Data

The national parks : shaping the system / produced by Harpers Ferry Center.
p. cm.
Rev. ed. of: The national parks / Barry Mackintosh. 1991.
Includes bibliographical references and index.
ISBN 10: 0-912627-73-5
ISBN 13: 978-0-912627-73-1 (alk. paper)
1. United States. National Park Service—History. 2. National parks and reserves—United States—History. I. Mackintosh, Barry. National parks. II. Harpers Ferry Center (U.S.)
SB482.A4N37252 2005
333.78'3'0973—dc22
2004030517

Campsite along the Potomac River at Wakefield, Virginia, 1924. George Washington Birthplace National Monument was established here six years later.

Part 1

George Grant, the National Park Service's first chief photographer, documented this duo of American bison at Wind Cave National Park, South Dakota, in 1936.

Introduction

A Few Words About This Book

When did the National Park System begin? The usual response is 1872, when an act of Congress created Yellowstone National Park, the first place so titled. Like a river formed from several branches, however, the System cannot be traced to a single source. Other components—the parks of the Nation's Capital, Hot Springs, parts of Yosemite—preceded Yellowstone as parklands reserved or established by the Federal Government. And there was no real "system" of national parks until Congress created a federal bureau, the National Park Service (NPS), in 1916 to manage those areas assigned to the U.S. Department of the Interior.

The systematic park administration within Interior paved the way for annexation of comparable areas from other federal agencies. In a 1933 government reorganization, the National Park Service acquired the War Department's national military parks and monuments, the Agriculture Department's national monuments, and the national capital parks. Thereafter the NPS would be the primary federal agency preserving and providing for public enjoyment of America's most significant natural and cultural properties in a fully comprehensive National Park System.

Ronald F. Lee's *Family Tree of the National Park System*, published by the Eastern National Park and Monument Association in 1972, chronicled the System's evolution to that date. Its usefulness led the NPS to issue a revised and expanded account titled *The National Parks: Shaping the System* in 1985. This is the third print edition of that publication, reflecting the System's continued growth and diversity.

The nomenclature of National Park System areas is often confusing. System units now bear some 30 titles besides "national park," which commonly identifies the largest, most spectacular natural areas. Other designations such as national seashore, national lakeshore, national river, and national scenic trail are usefully descriptive. In contrast, the national monument title—applied impartially to large natural areas like Dinosaur and small cultural sites like the Statue of Liberty—says little about a place. For no obvious reason, some historic forts are national monuments and others are national historic sites, while battlefields are variously titled national military parks, national battlefields, and national battlefield parks, among other things.

All these designations are rooted in the System's legislative and administrative history. Where distinctions in title denote no real differences in character or management policy, the differing designations usually reflect changes in fashion over time. Historical areas that once would have been named national monuments, for example, more recently have been titled national historic sites, if small, or national historical parks, if larger. Regardless of their titles, all System units are referred to generically as "parks," a practice followed in this book.

The dates used here for parks are usually those of the earliest laws, Presidential proclamations, or departmental orders authorizing or establishing them. In some cases these actions occurred before the areas were placed under NPS administration and thus in the National Park System. In 1970 Congress defined the System as including "any area of land and water now or hereafter administered by the Secretary of the Interior, through the National Park Service, for park, monument, historic, parkway, recreational, or other purposes." This legal definition excludes a number of national historic sites, memorials, trails, and other areas assisted or coordinated, but not administered, by the NPS.

Lee's *Family Tree*, with its chronological listing of park additions and concise discussion of significant examples, developments, and trends, was a valuable orientation and reference tool for NPS personnel and others tracking the System's growth to Yellowstone's centennial year. It is hoped that this revised edition of *Shaping the System*, still owing much to Lee's work, will serve the same purposes for the present generation of park employees and friends.

Old Faithful, shown here in winter 1953, is one of many geothermal wonders that draw worldwide attention. It helped lead to the creation of Yellowstone National Park.

Part 2

President Theodore Roosevelt *(left)* and John Muir at Glacier Point in Yosemite National Park, ca. 1903.

Shaping the System

Before the National Park Service

National Parks

The national park idea—the concept of large-scale natural preservation for public enjoyment—has been credited to the artist George Catlin, best known for his paintings of American Indians. On a trip to the Dakota region in 1832, he worried about the destructive effects of America's westward expansion on Indian civilization, wildlife, and wilderness. They might be preserved, he wrote, "by some great protecting policy of government . . . in a magnificent park. . . . a nation's park, containing man and beast, in all the wild[ness] and freshness of their nature's beauty!"

Catlin's vision of perpetuating indigenous cultures in this fashion was surely impractical, and his proposal had no immediate effect. Increasingly, however, romantic portrayals of nature by writers like James Fenimore Cooper and Henry David Thoreau and painters like Thomas Cole and Frederick Edwin Church would compete with older views of wilderness as something to be overcome. As appreciation for unspoiled nature grew and as spectacular natural areas in the American West were publicized, notions of preserving such places began to be taken seriously.

One such place was Yosemite Valley, where the national park idea came to partial fruition in 1864. In response to the desires of "various gentlemen of California, gentlemen of fortune, of taste, and of refinement," Sen. John Conness of California sponsored legislation to transfer the federally owned valley and nearby Mariposa Big Tree Grove to the state so they might "be used and preserved for the benefit of mankind." The act of Congress, signed by President Abraham Lincoln on June 30, granted California the lands on condition that they would "be held for public use, resort, and recreation . . . inalienable for all time."

The geological wonders of the Yellowstone region, in the Montana and Wyoming territories, remained little known until 1869–71, when successive expeditions led by David E. Folsom, Henry D. Washburn, and Ferdinand V. Hayden traversed the area and publicized their remarkable findings. Several members of these parties suggested reserving Yellowstone for public use rather than allowing it to fall under private control. The park idea received influential support from agents of the Northern Pacific Railroad Company, whose projected main line through Montana stood to benefit from a major tourist destination in the vicinity.

Yosemite was cited as a precedent, but differences in the two situations required different solutions. The primary access to Yellowstone was through Montana, and Montanans were among the leading park advocates. Most of Yellowstone lay in Wyoming, however, and neither Montana nor Wyoming was yet a state. So the park legislation, introduced in December 1871 by Senate Public Lands Committee Chairman Samuel C. Pomeroy of Kansas, was written to leave Yellowstone in federal custody.

The Yellowstone bill encountered some opposition from congressmen who questioned the propriety of such a large reservation. "The geysers will remain, no matter where the ownership of the land may be, and I do not know why settlers should be excluded from a tract of land forty miles square . . . in the Rocky mountains or any other place," complained Sen. Cornelius Cole of California. But most were persuaded otherwise. The bill passed Congress, and on March 1, 1872, President Ulysses S. Grant signed it into law.

The Yellowstone act withdrew more than two million acres of the public domain from settlement, occupancy, or sale to be "dedicated and set apart as a public park or pleasuring-ground for the benefit and enjoyment of the people." It placed the park "under the exclusive control of the Secretary of the Interior" who was charged to "provide for the preservation, from injury or spoliation, of all timber, mineral deposits, natural curiosities, or wonders within said park, and their retention in their natural condition." The Secretary was also to prevent the "wanton destruction" and commercial taking of fish and game—problems addressed more firmly by the Lacey Act of 1894, which prohibited hunting outright and set penalties for offenders.

With Yellowstone's establishment, the precedent was set for other natural reserves under federal jurisdiction. An 1875 act of Congress made most of Mackinac Island in Michigan a national park. Because

William Henry Jackson photographed an unidentified man on the Mammoth Hot Springs terraces at Yellowstone, 1871.

of the Army's presence there at Fort Mackinac, the Secretary of War was given responsibility for it. Mackinac National Park would survive only 20 years as such: when the fort was decommissioned in 1895, Congress transferred the federal lands on the island to Michigan for a state park.

The next great scenic national parks—Sequoia, General Grant, and Yosemite, all in California—did not come about until 1890, 18 years after Yellowstone. The initial Sequoia legislation, signed by President Benjamin Harrison on September 25, again followed that for Yellowstone in establishing "a public park, or pleasure ground, for the benefit and enjoyment of the people." Another act approved October 1 set aside General Grant, Yosemite, and a large addition to Sequoia as "reserved forest lands" but directed their management along park lines. Sequoia, General Grant (later incorporated in Kings Canyon National Park), and Yosemite were given their names by the Secretary of the Interior. Yosemite Valley and the Mariposa Grove remained under state administration until 1906, when they were returned to federal control and incorporated in Yosemite National Park.

In the Forest Reserve Act of 1891, Congress authorized U.S. Presidents to proclaim permanent forest reserves on the public domain. Forest reserves were retitled national forests in 1907, to be managed for long-term economic productivity under multiple-use conservation principles. Within 16 years Presidents Grover Cleveland, William McKinley, and Theodore Roosevelt proclaimed 159 national forests comprising more than 150 million acres. William Howard Taft and Woodrow Wilson added another 26 million acres by 1916.

National parks, preserved largely for their aesthetic qualities, demonstrated a greater willingness to forego economic gain. Congress thus maintained direct control over the establishment of parks and frequently had to be assured that the lands in question were worthless for other purposes. Park bills were usually enacted only after long and vigorous campaigns by their supporters. Such campaigns were not driven solely by preservationist ideals: as with Yellowstone, western railroads regularly lobbied for the early parks and built grand rustic hotels in them to boost their passenger business.

Mount Rainier National Park in Washington was the next of its kind, reserved in 1899. Nine more parks were established through 1916, including such scenic gems as Crater Lake in Oregon, Glacier in Montana, Rocky Mountain in Colorado, and Hawaii in the Hawaiian Islands. There were as yet no clear standards for national parks, however, and a few suffered by comparison. Among them was Sullys Hill, an undistinguished tract in North Dakota that was later transferred to the Agriculture Department as a game preserve.

The Secretary of the Interior was supposed to preserve and protect the parks, but early depredations by poachers and vandals at Yellowstone revealed the difficulties to be faced in managing these remote areas. In 1883 Congress authorized him to call on the Secretary of War for assistance, and three years later he did so, obtaining a cavalry detail to enforce Yellowstone's regulations and army engineers to develop park roads and buildings. Although the military presence was extended to Sequoia, General Grant, and Yosemite in 1891, the later parks received civilian superintendents and rangers.

National Monuments

While the early national parks were being established, a separate movement arose to protect the prehistoric cliff dwellings, pueblo remains, and early missions found by cowboys, army officers, ethnologists, and other explorers on the vast public lands of the Southwest. Efforts to secure protective legislation began among historically minded scientists and civic leaders in Boston and spread to similar circles in other cities during the 1880s and 1890s.

Congress took a first step in this direction in 1889 by authorizing the President to reserve from settlement or sale the land in Arizona containing the massive Casa Grande site. President Benjamin Harrison ordered the Casa Grande Ruin Reservation three years later. In 1904, at the request of the Interior Department's General Land Office, archeologist Edgar Lee Hewett reviewed prehistoric features on federal lands in Arizona, New Mexico, Colorado, and Utah and recommended specific sites for protection. The following year he drafted general legislation for the purpose. Strongly supported by Rep. John F. Lacey of Iowa, chairman of the House Public Lands Committee, it passed Congress and received President Theodore Roosevelt's signature on June 8, 1906.

Comparable to the Forest Reserve Act of 1891, the Antiquities Act of 1906 was a blanket authority for Presidents to proclaim and reserve "historic landmarks, historic and prehistoric structures, and other objects of historic or scientific interest" on lands owned or controlled by the United States as "national monuments." It also prohibited the excavation or appropriation of antiquities on federal lands without permission from the department having jurisdiction.

Separate legislation to protect the spectacular cliff dwellings of southwestern Colorado moved through Congress simultaneously, resulting in the creation of Mesa Verde National Park three weeks later. Thereafter the Antiquities Act was widely used to reserve such cultural features—and natural features as well. Roosevelt proclaimed 18 national monuments before leaving office in March 1909, 12 of which fell in the latter category. The first was Devils Tower in northeastern Wyoming, a massive stone shaft of volcanic origin, proclaimed September 24, 1906. The next three monuments followed that December: El Morro in New Mexico, site of prehistoric petroglyphs and historic inscriptions left by Spanish explorers and American pioneers; Montezuma Castle in Arizona, a well-preserved cliff dwelling; and Petrified Forest in Arizona.

National monuments were proclaimed on lands administered by the Agriculture and War departments as well as Interior. Proclamations before 1933 entailed no change of administration; a monument reserved under Agriculture or War would normally remain there unless Congress later made it or included it in a national park. In 1908, broadly construing the Antiquities Act's provision for "objects of scientific interest," Roosevelt proclaimed part of Arizona's Grand Canyon a national monument. Because the monument lay within a national forest, the Agriculture Department's Forest Service retained jurisdiction until 1919, when Congress established a larger Grand Canyon National Park in its place and assigned management responsibility to Interior's National Park Service. Similarly, Lassen Peak and Cinder Cone national monuments in California, proclaimed in 1907 under Forest Service jurisdiction, moved to Interior in 1916 when Lassen Volcanic National Park was established and encompassed both areas.

By the beginning of the 21st century, U.S. Presidents had proclaimed more than 100 national monuments. Although many were later incorporated in national parks or otherwise redesignated, and several were abolished, it may be said that nearly a quarter of the units of today's System sprang in whole or part from the Antiquities Act.

Mineral Springs
Two mineral spring reservations also contributed to the emerging National Park System. The first preceded all other components of the System outside the Nation's Capital.

"Taking the cure" at mineral spring resorts became highly fashionable in Europe during the 18th and 19th centuries, when thousands visited such famous spas as Bath, Aix-les-Bains, Aachen, Baden-Baden, and Karlsbad (Karlovy Vary). As mineral springs were found in America, they too attracted attention. Places like Saratoga Springs in New York and White Sulphur Springs in Virginia (now West Virginia) were developed privately, but Congress acted to maintain federal control of two springs west of the Mississippi.

Hot Springs in Arkansas Territory comprised 47 springs of salubrious repute emerging from a fault at the base of a mountain. In 1832

Congress reserved four sections of land containing Hot Springs "for the future disposal of the United States." After the Civil War the Interior Department permitted private entrepreneurs to build and operate bathhouses to which the spring waters were piped, and the Hot Springs Reservation became a popular resort.

In 1902 the Federal Government purchased 32 mineral springs near Sulphur, Oklahoma Territory, from the Choctaw and Chickasaw nations to create the Sulphur Springs Reservation, also under Interior's jurisdiction. The reservation was enlarged in 1904, and two years later Congress renamed it Platt National Park after the recently deceased Sen. Orville Platt of Connecticut, who had been active in Indian affairs.

Congress redesignated Hot Springs Reservation a national park in 1921. Although the park encompassed some natural terrain, it remained more an urbanized spa than a natural area. Platt, an equally anomalous national park, lost that designation in 1976 when it was incorporated in the new Chickasaw National Recreation Area.

An undated photograph depicts the "interior of a modern bathhouse" at Hot Springs National Park in Arkansas.

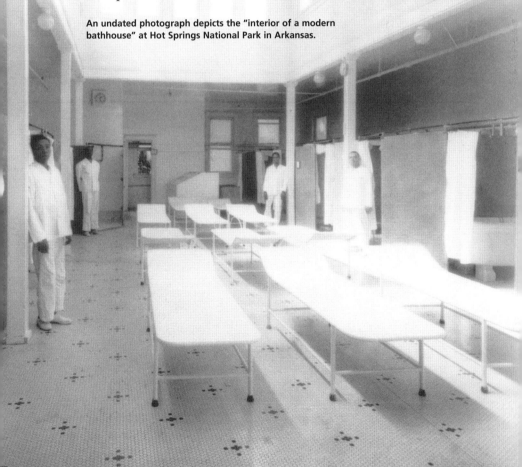

1832	April 20	Hot Springs Reservation, Arkansas (redesignated Hot Springs NP 1921)
1872	March 1	Yellowstone NP, Wyoming, Montana, and Idaho
1875	March 3	Mackinac NP, Michigan (transferred to state of Michigan 1895)
1889	March 2	Casa Grande Ruin Reservation, Arizona (redesignated Casa Grande NM 1918; redesignated Casa Grande Ruins NM 1926)
1890	Sept. 25	Sequoia NP, California
	Oct. 1	General Grant NP, California (incorporated in Kings Canyon NP 1940)
	Oct. 1	Yosemite NP, California
1899	March 2	Mount Rainier NP, Washington
1902	May 22	Crater Lake NP, Oregon
	July 1	Sulphur Springs Reservation, Oklahoma (redesignated Platt NP 1906; incorporated in Chickasaw NRA 1976)
1903	Jan. 9	Wind Cave NP, South Dakota
1904	April 27	Sullys Hill NP, North Dakota (transferred to Agriculture Dept. as game preserve 1931)
1906	June 8	*Antiquities Act*
	June 29	Mesa Verde NP, Colorado
	Sept. 24	Devils Tower NM, Wyoming
	Dec. 8	El Morro NM, New Mexico
	Dec. 8	Montezuma Castle NM, Arizona
	Dec. 8	Petrified Forest NM, Arizona (redesignated a NP 1962)
1907	March 11	Chaco Canyon NM, New Mexico (incorporated in Chaco Culture NHP 1980)
1908	Jan. 9	Muir Woods NM, California
	April 16	Natural Bridges NM, Utah
	May 11	Lewis and Clark Cavern NM, Montana (abolished 1937)
	Sept. 15	Tumacacori NM, Arizona (incorporated in Tumacacori NHP 1990)
1909	March 20	Navajo NM, Arizona
	July 31	Mukuntuweap NM, Utah (incorporated in Zion NM 1918)
	Sept. 21	Shoshone Cavern NM, Wyoming (abolished 1954)
	Nov. 1	Gran Quivira NM, New Mexico (incorporated in Salinas Pueblo Missions NM 1980)
1910	March 23	Sitka NM, Alaska (redesignated a NHP 1972)
	May 11	Glacier NP, Montana

1910	May 30	Rainbow Bridge NM, Utah
	Dec. 12	Pinnacles NM, California (date transferred from Agriculture Dept., where proclaimed 1908)
1911	May 24	Colorado NM, Colorado
1914	Jan. 31	Papago Saguaro NM, Arizona (abolished 1930)
1915	Jan. 26	Rocky Mountain NP, Colorado
	Oct. 4	Dinosaur NM, Colorado and Utah
1916	July 8	Sieur de Monts NM, Maine (redesignated Lafayette NP 1919; redesignated Acadia NP 1929)
	Aug. 1	Hawaii NP, Hawaii (split into Haleakalā NP and Hawaii NP 1960; latter redesignated Hawai'i Volcanoes NP 1961)
	Aug. 9	Capulin Mountain NM, New Mexico (redesignated Capulin Volcano NM 1987)
	Aug. 9	Lassen Volcanic NP, California (incorporated 1907 Cinder Cone and Lassen Peak NMs from Agriculture Dept.)
	Aug. 25	*National Park Service Act*

IHS International Historic Site	**NM** National Monument	**NRRA** National River and Recreation Area
NB National Battlefield	**NM & PRES** National Monument and Preserve	**N RES** National Reserve
NBP National Battlefield Park	**N MEM** National Memorial	**NS** National Seashore
NBS National Battlefield Site	**NMP** National Military Park	**NSR** National Scenic River/Riverway
NHP National Historical Park	**NP** National Park	**NST** National Scenic Trail
NHP & PRES National Historical Park and Preserve	**NP & PRES** National Park and Preserve	**PKWY** Parkway
NH RES National Historical Reserve	**N PRES** National Preserve	**SRR** Scenic and Recreational River
NHS National Historic Site	**NR** National River	**WR** Wild River
NL National Lakeshore	**NRA** National Recreation Area	**WSR** Wild and Scenic River

Forging a System, 1916 to 1933

By August 1916 the Department of the Interior oversaw 14 national parks, 21 national monuments, and the Hot Springs and Casa Grande Ruin reservations. This collection of areas was not a true park system, however, for it lacked systematic management. Without an organization equipped for the purpose, Interior Secretaries had been forced to call on the Army to develop and police Yellowstone and the parks in California. The troops protected these areas and served their visitors well for the most part, but their primary mission lay elsewhere, and their continued presence could not be counted on. Civilian appointees of varying capabilities managed the other national parks, while most of the national monuments received minimal attention from part-time custodians. In the absence of an effective central administration, those in charge operated with little coordinated supervision or policy guidance.

Lacking unified leadership, the parks were also vulnerable to competing interests. Conservationists of the utilitarian school, who advocated the regulated use of natural resources to achieve "the greatest good for the greatest number," championed the construction of dams by public authorities for water supply, electric power, and irrigation purposes. When the city of San Francisco sought permission to dam Hetch Hetchy Valley in Yosemite National Park for its water supply in the first decade of the 20th century, the utilitarian and preservationist wings of the conservation movement came to blows. Over the passionate opposition of John Muir and other park supporters, Congress in 1913 approved what historian John Ise later called "the worst disaster ever to come to any national park."

"The rape of Hetch Hetchy," as the preservationists termed it, highlighted the institutional weakness of the park movement. While utilitarian conservation had become well represented in government by the U.S. Geological Survey (established in 1879), the Forest Service (1905), and the Reclamation Service (1907), no comparable bureau spoke for park preservation in Washington. The need for an organization to operate the parks and advocate their interests was clearer than ever.

Among those recognizing this need was Stephen T. Mather, a wealthy Chicago businessman, vigorous outdoorsman, and born promoter.

In 1914 Mather complained to Interior Secretary Franklin K. Lane, a fellow alumnus of the University of California at Berkeley, about the mismanagement of the parks. Lane invited Mather to come to Washington and do something about it. Mather accepted the challenge, arriving early in 1915 to become assistant to the Secretary for park matters. Twenty-five-year-old Horace M. Albright, another Berkeley graduate who had recently joined the Interior Department, became Mather's top aide.

Previous efforts to establish a national parks bureau in Interior had been resisted by the Agriculture Department's Forest Service, which rightly foresaw the creation and removal of more parks from its national forests. Lobbying skillfully to overcome such opposition Mather and Albright blurred the distinction between utilitarian conservation and preservation by emphasizing the economic potential of parks as tourist meccas.

A vigorous public relations campaign led to supportive articles in *National Geographic*, *The Saturday Evening Post*, and other popular magazines. Mather hired his own publicist and obtained funds from 17 western railroads to produce *The National Parks Portfolio*, a lavishly illustrated publication sent to congressmen and other civic leaders. Congress responded as desired, and on August 25, 1916, President Woodrow Wilson affixed his signature to the bill creating the National Park Service. The National Park Service Act made the new bureau responsible for the 35 national parks and monuments then under Interior, Hot Springs Reservation, and "such other national parks and reservations of like character as may be hereafter created by Congress." In managing these areas the NPS was directed "to conserve the scenery and the natural and historic objects and the wild life therein and to provide for the enjoyment of the same in such manner and by such means as will leave them unimpaired for the enjoyment of future generations."

Lane appointed Mather the Service's first director. Albright served as assistant director until 1919, then as superintendent of Yellow-

Stephen T. Mather, the first director of the National Park Service, at Glacier Point in Yosemite National Park, 1926.

stone and field assistant director before succeeding Mather in 1929. Mather was initially incapacitated by illness, leaving Albright to organize the bureau in 1917, obtain its first appropriations from Congress, and prepare its first park policies.

The policies, issued in a May 13, 1918, letter from Lane to Mather, elaborated on the Service's mission of conserving park resources and providing for their enjoyment by the public. "Every activity of the Service is subordinate to the duties imposed upon it to faithfully preserve the parks for posterity in essentially their natural state," the letter stated.

At the same time, it reflected Mather and Albright's conviction that more visitors must be attracted and accommodated if the parks and the NPS were to prosper. Automobiles, not permitted in Yellowstone until 1915, were to be allowed in all parks. "Low-priced camps . . . as well as comfortable and even luxurious hotels" would be provided by concessioners. Mountain climbing, horseback riding, swimming, boating, fishing, and winter sports would be encouraged, as would natural history museums, exhibits, and other activities furthering the educational value of the parks.

The policy letter also sought to guide further expansion of the System: "In studying new park projects, you should seek to find scenery of supreme and distinctive quality or some natural feature so extraordinary or unique as to be of national interest and importance. . . . The national park system as now constituted should not be lowered in standard, dignity, and prestige by the inclusion of areas which express in less than the highest terms the particular class or kind of exhibit which they represent."

The first national park following establishment of the National Park Service was Mount McKinley in Alaska, reserved in 1917 to protect the mountain sheep, caribou, moose, bears, and other wildlife on and around North America's highest mountain. The incomparable Grand Canyon National Park, incorporating the Forest Service's Grand Canyon National Monument, followed in 1919. Other national parks established through 1933 included Lafayette, Maine, in 1919 (renamed Acadia in 1929); Zion, Utah, in 1919; Utah in that state in 1924 (renamed Bryce Canyon in 1928); Grand Teton, Wyoming, in 1929; and Carlsbad Caverns, New Mexico, in 1930. Like Grand Canyon, all these except Grand Teton incorporated earlier national monuments.

Casa Grande Ruin Reservation remained under Interior's General Land Office until 1918, when it was proclaimed a national monument and reassigned to the NPS. Two Alaska monuments proclaimed during the period, Katmai and Glacier Bay, were each larger than any national park and until 1978 were the System's largest areas. Katmai, established in 1918, protected the scene of a major volcanic eruption six years before. Glacier Bay, established in 1925, contained numerous tidewater glaciers and their mountain setting. Congress made both of them national parks in 1980. Badlands National Monument, South Dakota, and Arches National Monument, Utah, both established in 1929, became national parks in the 1970s.

Badlands was the first national monument established directly by an act of Congress rather than by a Presidential proclamation under the Antiquities Act. By the beginning of the 21st century Congress had established more than three dozen national monuments, although about a third of them no longer retained that designation.

Through the 1920s the National Park System was really a western park system. Of the Service's holdings, only Lafayette (Acadia) National Park in Maine lay east of the Mississippi. This geographic bias was hardly surprising: the West was the setting for America's most spectacular natural scenery, and most of the land there was federally owned—subject to park or monument reservation without purchase. If the System were to benefit more people and maximize its support in Congress, however, it would have to expand eastward—a foremost objective of NPS leadership.

In 1926 Congress authorized Shenandoah, Great Smoky Mountains, and Mammoth Cave national parks in the Appalachian region but required that their lands be donated. John D. Rockefeller, Jr., who gave more than $3 million for lands and roads for Acadia, contributed more than $5 million for Great Smoky Mountains and a lesser amount for Shenandoah. With such private assistance, the states involved gradually acquired and turned over the lands needed to establish these large natural parks in the following decade.

But the Service's greatest opportunity in the East lay in another realm—that of history and historic sites. The War Department had been involved in preserving a range of historic battlefields, forts, and memorials there since the 1890s. Horace Albright, whose expansionist instincts were accompanied by a personal interest in history, sought the transfer of these areas to the NPS soon after its creation. He argued that the NPS was better equipped to interpret them to the public, but skeptics in the War Department and Congress questioned how the bureau's focus on western wilderness qualified it to run the military parks better than the military.

After succeeding Mather as director in 1929, Albright resumed his efforts. As a first step he got Congress to establish three new historical parks in the East under NPS administration: George Washington Birthplace National Monument at Wakefield, Virginia; Colonial Na-

tional Monument at Jamestown and Yorktown, Virginia; and Morristown National Historical Park in New Jersey, where Washington and
the Continental Army spent two winters during the Revolution.

Morristown, authorized March 2, 1933, was the first national historical park, a more descriptive designation that Congress would
apply to Colonial in 1936 and three dozen more historical areas
thereafter. Of more immediate significance, Colonial's Yorktown Battlefield and Morristown moved the NPS directly into military history,
advancing its case for the War Department's areas. They would not
be long in coming.

A highlight for visitors in Mammoth Cave National Park's
early days, floating excursions on the underground Echo
River were eventually discontinued to protect the cave
system's ecological processes.

1917	Feb. 26	Mount McKinley NP, Alaska (incorporated in Denali NP and N PRES 1980)
	June 29	Verendrye NM, North Dakota (abolished 1956)
1918	March 18	Zion NM, Utah (incorporated Mukuntuweap NM; redesignated a NP 1919)
	Aug. 3	Casa Grande NM, Arizona (Casa Grande Ruin Reservation redesignated and transferred from General Land Office; redesignated Casa Grande Ruins NM 1926)
	Sept. 24	Katmai NM, Alaska (incorporated in Katmai NP and N PRES 1980)
1919	Feb. 26	Grand Canyon NP, Arizona (incorporated 1908 Grand Canyon NM from Agriculture Dept.)
	Dec. 12	Scotts Bluff NM, Nebraska
	Dec. 12	Yucca House NM, Colorado
1922	Oct. 21	Fossil Cycad NM, South Dakota (abolished 1956)
1923	Jan. 24	Aztec Ruin NM, New Mexico (redesignated Aztec Ruins NM 1928)
	March 2	Hovenweep NM, Colorado and Utah
	May 31	Pipe Spring NM, Arizona
	Oct. 25	Carlsbad Cave NM, New Mexico (redesignated Carlsbad Caverns NP 1930)
1924	May 2	Craters of the Moon NM, Idaho
	June 7	Utah NP, Utah (1923 Bryce Canyon NM redesignated and transferred from Agriculture Dept.; redesignated Bryce Canyon NP 1928)
	Dec. 9	Wupatki NM, Arizona
1925	Feb. 26	Glacier Bay NM, Alaska (incorporated in Glacier Bay NP and N PRES 1980)
	Nov. 21	Lava Beds NM, California
1926	May 22	Great Smoky Mountains NP, North Carolina and Tennessee
	May 22	Shenandoah NP, Virginia
	May 25	Mammoth Cave NP, Kentucky
1929	Feb. 26	Grand Teton NP, Wyoming
	March 4	Badlands NM, South Dakota (redesignated a NP 1978)
	April 12	Arches NM, Utah (redesignated a NP 1971)
1930	Jan. 23	George Washington Birthplace NM, Virginia
	July 3	Colonial NM, Virginia (redesignated a NHP 1936)
1931	Feb. 14	Canyon de Chelly NM, Arizona
	March 3	Isle Royale NP, Michigan

1932	Feb. 25	Bandelier NM, New Mexico (date transferred from Agriculture Dept., where proclaimed 1916)
	March 17	Great Sand Dunes NM, Colorado (redesignated a NP 2000)
	Dec. 22	Second Grand Canyon NM, Arizona (incorporated in Grand Canyon NP 1975)
1933	Jan. 18	White Sands NM, New Mexico
	Feb. 11	Death Valley NM, California and Nevada (incorporated in Death Valley NP 1994)
	March 2	Black Canyon of the Gunnison NM, Colorado (redesignated a NP 1999)
	March 2	Morristown NHP, New Jersey
	Aug. 10	*Reorganization*

IHS   International Historic Site
NB   National Battlefield
NBP   National Battlefield Park
NBS   National Battlefield Site
NHP   National Historical Park
NHP & PRES   National Historical Park and Preserve
NH RES   National Historical Reserve
NHS   National Historic Site
NL   National Lakeshore

NM   National Monument
NM & PRES   National Monument and Preserve
N MEM   National Memorial
NMP   National Military Park
NP   National Park
NP & PRES   National Park and Preserve
N PRES   National Preserve
NR   National River
NRA   National Recreation Area

NRRA   National River and Recreation Area
N RES   National Reserve
NS   National Seashore
NSR   National Scenic River/Riverway
NST   National Scenic Trail
PKWY   Parkway
SRR   Scenic and Recreational River
WR   Wild River
WSR   Wild and Scenic River

The Reorganization of 1933

On March 3, 1933, President Herbert Hoover approved legislation authorizing Presidents to reorganize the executive branch of the government. He had no time to take advantage of the new authority, for he would leave office the next day. The beneficiary was his successor Franklin D. Roosevelt.

Hoover had arranged to give the government his fishing retreat on the Rapidan River in Virginia for inclusion in Shenandoah National Park. On April 9 Roosevelt motored there to inspect the property for his possible use. Horace Albright accompanied the party and was invited to sit behind the President on the return drive. As they passed through Civil War country, Albright turned the conversation to history and mentioned his desire to acquire the War Department's historical areas. Roosevelt readily agreed and directed him to initiate an executive order for the transfer.

Roosevelt's order—actually two orders signed June 10 and July 28, effective August 10—did what Albright had asked and more. Not only did the National Park Service receive the War Department's parks and monuments, it achieved another longtime objective by getting the national monuments then held by the Forest Service and responsibility for virtually all monuments created thereafter until the 1990s. It also took over the National Capital Parks, then managed by a separate office in Washington. When the dust settled, the Service's previous holdings had been joined by a dozen predominantly natural areas in eight western states and the District of Columbia and 44 historical areas in the District and 18 states, 13 of them east of the Mississippi.

The reorganization of August 10, 1933, was arguably the most significant event in the evolution of the National Park System. There was now a single system of federal parklands, truly national in scope, embracing historic as well as natural places. The Service's major involvement with historic sites held limitless potential for the System's further growth.

Unlike the War Department, the NPS was not constrained to focus on military history but could seek areas representing all aspects of America's past. Management of the parks in the Nation's Capital would give the NPS high visibility with members of Congress and visitors from around the Nation and invite expansion of the System

28

into other urban regions. Although the big western wilderness parks would still dominate, the bureau and its responsibilities would henceforth be far more diverse.

National Capital Parks

The parks of the Nation's Capital are the oldest elements of today's National Park System, dating from the creation of the District of Columbia in 1790-91. On July 16, 1790, President George Washington approved legislation empowering him to appoint three commissioners to lay out the District, "purchase or accept such quantity of land . . . as the President shall deem proper for the use of the United States," and provide suitable buildings for Congress, the President, and government offices. The next year Washington met with the proprietors of lands to be included in the federal city and signed a purchase agreement resulting in the acquisition of 17 reservations. In accordance with Pierre Charles L'Enfant's plan for the city, Reservation 1 became the site of the White House and the President's Park, including Lafayette Park and the Ellipse; Reservation 2 became the site of the Capitol and the Mall; and Reservation 3 became the site of the Washington Monument.

A century later the Nation's Capital park system received two major additions. Rock Creek Park, Washington's largest, was authorized by Congress on September 27, 1890—two days after Sequoia and four days before Yosemite. Some of the same legislative language that the California parks inherited from Yellowstone appeared in this act as well. Rock Creek Park was "dedicated and set apart as a public park or pleasure ground for the benefit and enjoyment of the people of the United States," and regulations were ordered to "provide for the preservation from injury or spoliation of all timber, animals, or curiosities within said park, and their retention in their natural condition, as nearly as possible." Its value as a preserved natural area increased with the growth of its urban environs (although the NPS has magnified its significance since 1975 by listing the park with its

Ceremonial pointing of the capstone of the Washington Monument, 1884.

California contemporaries as a discrete National Park System unit).

East and West Potomac parks, on the other hand, were artificially created on fill dredged from the Potomac River in the 1880s. In 1897 Congress reserved this large reclaimed area for park development, and in the 20th century it became the site of the Lincoln, Jefferson, and Franklin Delano Roosevelt memorials; Constitution Gardens; and the Vietnam Veterans and Korean War Veterans memorials, among other features.

The last major addition to the Nation's Capital park system before the reorganization was the George Washington Memorial Parkway. A 1928 act of Congress authorized the Mount Vernon Memorial Highway, linking the planned Arlington Memorial Bridge and Mount Vernon, to be completed for the bicentennial of Washington's birth in 1932. In 1930 Congress incorporated the highway in a greatly enlarged George Washington Memorial Parkway project, which entailed extensive land acquisition and scenic roadways on both sides of the Potomac River from Mount Vernon upstream to Great Falls. Although never fully completed as planned, the project proceeded far enough by the 1960s to buffer significant stretches of the river with parkland.

The parks of the Nation's Capital were managed by a succession of administrators, beginning with the commissioners appointed by President Washington to establish the federal city. From 1802 to 1867 the city's public buildings and grounds were under a superintendent and then a commissioner of public buildings, who reported to the Secretary of the Interior after the Interior Department was established in 1849. In 1867 the parks and buildings were turned over to the chief engineer of the Army. His Office of Public Buildings and Grounds ran them until 1925, when it was succeeded by the Office of Public Buildings and Public Parks of the National Capital. The latter office, still headed by an army engineer officer but directly under the President, lasted until the 1933 reorganization. Its responsibility for federal buildings as well as parks passed to the National Park Service, which was renamed the Office of National Parks, Buildings, and Reservations in Roosevelt's executive orders. The bureau carried this unwieldy title for less than seven months, regaining its old name in a March 2, 1934, appropriations act; but it did not shed the public buildings function until 1939.

The term National Capital Parks (usually capitalized) has been variously used since the reorganization as a collective designation for the national parklands in and around Washington and as the name of the NPS office managing them. Today National Capital Parks officially denotes only those miscellaneous parklands in the District of Columbia and nearby Maryland not classed as discrete units of the National Park System. The designation thus excludes the major Presidential and war memorials and certain other NPS-administered properties in the Washington area. But it is often used informally to encompass them as well.

National Memorials

National memorials in and outside Washington formed the most distinctly different class of areas added in the reorganization. Among them are such great national symbols as the Washington Monument and the Statue of Liberty. Although these and several other National Park System memorials bear other designations, they qualify as memorials because they were not directly associated with the people or events they commemorate but were built by later generations.

The first federal action toward a national memorial now in the System came in 1783, when the Continental Congress resolved "that an equestrian statue of General Washington be erected where the residence of Congress shall be established." L'Enfant's plan for the city of Washington provided a prominent location for the statue, but Congress provided no funds for it. A private organization, the Washington National Monument Society, acquired the site and began construction of an obelisk in 1848, but its resources proved inadequate. Not until 1876, the centennial of American independence, did the government assume responsibility for completing and maintaining the Washington Monument. Army engineers finished it in accordance with a simplified design, and it was dedicated in 1885.

During the centennial France offered the Statue of Liberty as a gift to the United States. Congress authorized acceptance of the statue, provision of a suitable site in New York Harbor, and preservation of the structure "as a monument of art and the continued good will of the great nation which aided us in our struggle for freedom." In effect a memorial to the Franco-American alliance during the Revolution, the Statue of Liberty was dedicated in 1886. President Calvin Coolidge proclaimed it a national monument under the War Department, its custodian, in 1924.

In 1911 Congress authorized construction of the Lincoln Memorial in Washington's Potomac Park, directly aligned with the Capitol and the Washington Monument. The completed masterpiece of architect Henry Bacon and sculptor Daniel Chester French was dedicated in 1922. Another classical memorial to Lincoln, enshrining his supposed birthplace cabin at Hodgenville, Kentucky, had been privately erected in 1907–11 from a design by John Russell Pope, architect of the later Thomas Jefferson Memorial in Washington. The birthplace property was given to the United States in 1916 and administered by the War Department as Abraham Lincoln National Park. It was ultimately redesignated a national historic site after it came under the National Park Service, but the character of its development makes it in effect a memorial.

Other memorials authorized by Congress before 1933 included one to Portuguese explorer Juan Rodriguez Cabrillo in San Diego, proclaimed Cabrillo National Monument under the War Department in 1913; Perry's Victory Memorial, Ohio, in 1919; Mount Rushmore National Memorial, South Dakota, in 1925; Kill Devil Hill Monument (later Wright Brothers National Memorial), North Carolina, in 1927; the George Rogers Clark Memorial in Vincennes, Indiana, in 1928; and Theodore Roosevelt Island in Washington, D.C., in 1932. Cabrillo National Monument and Kill Devil Hill Monument were transferred from the War Department and Theodore Roosevelt Island from the Office of Public Buildings and Public Parks of the National Capital in the reorganization, which also gave the NPS fiscal responsibility for the commissions developing the Mount Rushmore and George Rogers Clark memorials.

The NPS received Mount Rushmore itself in 1939 and the Clark memorial under a 1966 act of Congress authorizing George Rogers Clark National Historical Park. Several historic sites proposed for this park were never acquired, leaving it essentially a memorial area. The NPS had no responsibility for Perry's Victory Memorial, constructed by another commission, until 1936, when Congress authorized its addition to the National Park System as Perry's Victory and International Peace Memorial National Monument. The superfluous national monument suffix was dropped in 1972.

The Lee Mansion in Arlington, Virginia, transferred from the War Department in the reorganization, was ultimately retitled Arlington House, The Robert E. Lee Memorial, by Congress in 1972. (Because the house was directly associated with Lee and has been restored to the period of his occupancy, it would more appropriately be designated a national historic site.)

National Battlefields and Cemeteries
The first official step to commemorate an American battle where it occurred was taken in 1781. Inspired by the Franco-American victory over the British at Yorktown that October, the Continental Congress authorized "to be erected at York, Virginia, a marble column, adorned with emblems of the alliance between the United States and His Most Christian Majesty; and inscribed with a succinct narrative of the surrender." Funds were then unavailable, and Congress did

not follow through until the centennial of the surrender in 1881, when the Yorktown Column was raised as prescribed a century before. It is now a prominent feature of Colonial National Historical Park.

The battlefield monument idea received major impetus in 1823 when Daniel Webster, Edward Everett, and other prominent citizens formed the Bunker Hill Battle Monument Association to save part of Breed's Hill in Charlestown, Massachusetts, and erect a great obelisk on it. Webster delivered a moving oration before a large audience at the cornerstone laying in 1825, the 50th anniversary of the battle. The Bunker Hill Monument demonstrated how commemorative sentiment might be crystallized and was the prototype for many other battlefield monuments. During the centennial years of the Revolution, Congress appropriated funds to supplement local contributions for monuments at Bennington Battlefield, Saratoga, Newburgh, and Oriskany, New York; Kings Mountain, South Carolina; Monmouth, New Jersey; and Groton, Connecticut. Like the Yorktown Column, the Bunker Hill, Kings Mountain, and Saratoga monuments were later included in National Park System areas.

The "mystic chords of memory" elicited by such Revolutionary War monuments in both the North and the South helped draw the two sections together after the Civil War. Confederate veterans from South Carolina and Virginia participated in the Bunker Hill centennial in 1875, the first time former Union and Confederate troops publicly fraternized after the war. The practice of joint reunions later spread to Civil War battlefields, culminating in huge veterans' encampments at Gettysburg in 1888 and Chickamauga in 1889.

Even before the Civil War ended, Pennsylvania had chartered the Gettysburg Battlefield Memorial Association in 1864 to commemorate "the great deeds of valor . . . and the signal events which render these battle-grounds illustrious." A preservation society also began work at Chickamauga, Georgia, and Chattanooga, Tennessee. Prompted by veterans' organizations and others influential in such activities, Congress began in the 1890s to go beyond the battlefield monument concept to full-scale battlefield preservation.

On August 19, 1890, a month before establishing Sequoia National Park, Congress authorized Chickamauga and Chattanooga National Military Park. Three more national military parks followed before the century's end: Shiloh in 1894, Gettysburg in 1895, and Vicksburg in 1899. The War Department purchased and managed their lands, while participating states, military units, and associations provided

The New York State Monument, dedicated in 1919, rises above a battery at Antietam National Battlefield, Maryland.

monuments at appropriate locations. At Antietam, on the other hand, Congress provided for acquisition of only token lands where monuments and markers might be placed. It and other places where this less expansive policy was adopted were designated national battlefield sites. Antietam and most of the other national battlefield sites were later enlarged and retitled national battlefields.

The 1907 authorization of the Chalmette Monument and Grounds, commemorating the Battle of New Orleans during the War of 1812, departed from the recent focus on the Civil War. Guilford Courthouse National Military Park, North Carolina, authorized a decade later, encompassed the first Revolutionary War battlefield so preserved. Confronted with many more proposals, Congress in 1926 asked the War Department to survey all the nation's historic battlefields and make recommendations for their preservation or commemoration.

The results guided Congress in adding 11 more areas to the War Department's park system before the reorganization: the site of the opening engagement of the French and Indian War at Fort Necessity in Pennsylvania; the Revolutionary War battlefields of Cowpens and Kings Mountain in South Carolina and Moores Creek in North Carolina; and the Civil War sites of Appomattox Court House, Fredericksburg and Spotsylvania County, and Petersburg in Virginia, Brices Cross Roads and Tupelo in Mississippi, and Fort Donelson and Stones River in Tennessee.

Roosevelt's initial executive order of June 10, 1933, had provided for all the War Department's domestic national cemeteries to come to the NPS along with its battlefield parks. At Horace Albright's urging, this wholesale transfer was amended in the supplementary order of July 28 to include only 11 cemeteries associated with the battlefields or other NPS holdings: Antietam (Sharpsburg) National Cemetery, Maryland; Battleground National Cemetery, Washington, D.C.; Chattanooga National Cemetery, Tennessee (returned to the War Department in 1944); Fort Donelson (Dover) National Cemetery, Tennessee; Fredericksburg National Cemetery, Virginia; Gettysburg National Cemetery, Pennsylvania; Poplar Grove (Petersburg) National Cemetery, Virginia; Shiloh (Pittsburgh Landing) National Cemetery, Tennessee; Stones River (Murfreesboro) National Cemetery, Tennessee; Vicksburg National Cemetery, Mississippi; and Yorktown National Cemetery, Virginia.

Most famous among these is Gettysburg National Cemetery. The battle of Gettysburg was scarcely over when Gov. Andrew Y. Curtin of Pennsylvania hastened to the field to help care for the casualties. More than 3,500 Union soldiers had been killed in action; many were hastily interred in improvised graves. At Curtin's request, Gettysburg attorney David Wills purchased 17 acres and engaged William Saunders, an eminent horticulturalist, to lay out the grounds for a cemetery. Fourteen northern states provided the necessary funds. At the dedication on November 19, 1863, President Abraham Lincoln delivered his Gettysburg Address. Gettysburg National Cemetery became the property of the United States in 1872, 23 years before establishment of the adjoining national military park.

Similar events took place on the other great battlefields of the Civil War. Congress recognized the importance of caring for the remains of the Union war dead with general legislation in 1867 enabling the extensive national cemetery system developed by the War Department. As at Gettysburg, each of the battlefield cemeteries was carefully landscaped to achieve an effect of "simple grandeur," and each preceded establishment of its related battlefield park.

The 1867 act also led to preservation of an important battleground of the Indian wars. In 1879 the Secretary of War established a national cemetery on the Little Bighorn battlefield in Montana Territory, and in 1886 President Grover Cleveland reserved a square mile of the battlefield for what was then called the National Cemetery of Custer's Battlefield Reservation. The War Department transferred the reservation to the NPS in 1940. Congress retitled it Custer Battlefield National Monument in 1946 and Little Bighorn Battlefield National Monument in 1991. (To retain some titular recognition of Custer, the 1991 act also designated the cemetery within the monument Custer National Cemetery.)

Other national cemeteries acquired by the NPS after the reorganization were Andrew Johnson National Cemetery, part of Andrew Johnson National Monument, Tennessee, authorized in 1935; Chalmette National Cemetery, transferred from the War Department for Chalmette National Historical Park, Louisiana, in 1939; and Andersonville National Cemetery, part of Andersonville National Historic Site, Georgia, authorized in 1970.

Until 1975 the national cemeteries acquired in the reorganization were listed as separate units of the National Park System. Since then the cemeteries, while retaining their special identities, have been carried as components of their associated parks.

Other War Department Properties

As national monuments were being reserved under Interior Department jurisdiction, others were proclaimed on War and Agriculture department lands. Ten national monuments were on military reservations before their transfer to the NPS in 1933.

President William Howard Taft proclaimed the first War Department national monument, Big Hole Battlefield, Montana, in 1910 to protect the site of an 1877 battle between U.S. troops and Nez Perce Indians. Five later monuments resulted from a single proclamation by President Coolidge on October 15, 1924. Fort Marion National Monument, later retitled with its Spanish name Castillo de San Marcos, recognized an old Spanish fort in St. Augustine, Florida. Fort Matanzas National Monument protected an outpost built by the Spanish in 1742 to defend the southern approaches to St. Augustine. Fort Pulaski National Monument contained a brick fort built during the 1830s outside Savannah that had yielded under bombardment by Federal rifled cannon in 1862. The Statue of Liberty, based on Fort Wood in New York Harbor, became a national monument (to which Ellis Island was added in 1965). A small national monument for Castle Pinckney in Charleston Harbor was later abolished.

Two War Department areas acquired in the reorganization were then titled national parks. Abraham Lincoln National Park has been cited above in connection with memorials. The other was Fort McHenry in Baltimore. A 1925 act of Congress directed the Secretary of War "to begin the restoration of Fort McHenry . . . to such a condition as would make it suitable for preservation permanently as a national park and perpetual national memorial shrine as the birthplace of the immortal 'Star-Spangled Banner.'" Abraham Lincoln and Fort McHenry national parks received more appropriate designations after coming to the NPS, although the unique "national monument and historic shrine" label Congress gave the fort in 1939 might have been abridged.

Arlington, the estate across the Potomac from Washington, D.C., was inherited by Robert E. Lee's wife from her father, George Washington Parke Custis, in 1857. During the Civil War the Union Army occupied it and the War Department began what became Arlington National Cemetery on its grounds. Lee's national reputation rose in later years, and in 1925 Congress authorized the War Department to restore Arlington House (also termed the Lee Mansion and Custis-Lee Mansion) in his honor. After the mansion's transfer to the NPS it was managed with the National Capital Parks.

The 1930 act authorizing the George Washington Memorial Parkway directed that Fort Washington, a 19th-century fortification guarding the Potomac approach to the capital, should be added to the parkway holdings when no longer needed for military purposes. The War Department relinquished it to the NPS in 1940. Fort Washington Park has been classified as a separate unit of the National Park System since 1975.

Agriculture Department National Monuments

Twenty-one national monuments were proclaimed on national forest lands under the Department of Agriculture before the 1933 reorganization. The first two were Lassen Peak and Cinder Cone in Lassen Peak National Forest, proclaimed by Theodore Roosevelt on May 6, 1907, to protect evidence of what was then the most recent volcanic activity in the United States. As previously noted, they were transferred to the Interior Department in 1916 as the nuclei of Lassen Volcanic National Park.

Fourteen of Agriculture's other monuments were also established to preserve "scientific objects." Especially noteworthy was Roosevelt's 1908 proclamation of Grand Canyon National Monument, comprising 818,650 acres within Grand Canyon National Forest, to impede commercial development there. Roosevelt's bold action was later sustained by the U.S. Supreme Court, confirming the precedent for other vast monuments like Katmai, Glacier Bay, and Death Valley. The Grand Canyon monument was superseded by Grand Canyon National Park when the latter was established under NPS jurisdiction in 1919. (A second Grand Canyon National Monument, proclaimed in 1932 and assigned to the NPS, was incorporated in the national park in 1975.)

On March 2, 1909, two days before leaving office, Roosevelt proclaimed another large national monument, Mount Olympus in Olympic National Forest, Washington. Encompassing 615,000 acres, it was intended to protect the Roosevelt elk and important stands of Sitka spruce, western hemlock, Douglas fir, and Alaska cedar. It formed the nucleus for Olympic National Park in 1938.

The other natural monuments included four caves: Jewel Cave in South Dakota; Oregon Caves in Oregon; Lehman Caves in Nevada; and Timpanogos Cave in Utah. In the National Park System they would join Carlsbad Caverns, Mammoth Cave, and Wind Cave national parks (and two national monuments later abolished: Lewis and Clark Caverns, Montana, and Shoshone Cavern, Wyoming). The first of only five archeological monuments in the group was Gila Cliff Dwellings, New Mexico, proclaimed November 16, 1907. It was followed by Tonto and Walnut Canyon in Arizona and then by Bandelier, New Mexico, established within the Santa Fe National Forest in 1916. President Hoover enlarged Bandelier and reassigned it to the NPS in February 1932, a year and a half before the reorganization. The fifth was Old Kasaan National Monument, Alaska, abolished in 1955.

Grand Canyon National Park, Arizona, 1939.

A limited reversion to Agriculture Department administration of national monuments came on December 1, 1978, when President Jimmy Carter proclaimed the Admiralty Island and Misty Fjords national monuments within Tongass National Forest, Alaska, and ordered their retention by the Forest Service. Congress confirmed their status two years later. In 1982 Congress established Mount St. Helens National Volcanic Monument at the site of the recent eruption in Gifford Pinchot National Forest, Washington, and kept it under the Forest Service. It did the same with Newberry National Volcanic Monument, established in 1990 in Deschutes National Forest, Oregon.

Hollowed-out portions of these tufa cliffs at Bandelier National Monument formed the back walls of pueblo rooms; holes supported beams for the outer structure of the pueblo.

National Capital Parks, 1790–1933

1790	July 16	District of Columbia authorized, including National Capital Parks, National Mall, White House
1866	April 7	Ford's Theatre, District of Columbia (date acquisition authorized; designated a NHS 1970)
1890	Sept. 27	Rock Creek Park, District of Columbia
1896	June 11	House Where Lincoln Died, District of Columbia (date acquisition authorized; incorporated in Ford's Theatre NHS 1970)
1897	March 3	Potomac Park, District of Columbia (component of National Capital Parks)
1928	May 23	Mount Vernon Memorial Highway, Virginia (incorporated in George Washington Memorial PKWY 1930)
1930	May 29	George Washington Memorial PKWY, District of Columbia, Maryland, and Virginia

National Memorials, 1876–1933

1876	Aug. 2	Washington Monument, District of Columbia (date accepted by United States; dedicated 1885)
1877	March 3	Statue of Liberty, New York (date accepted by United States; dedicated 1886; also listed with Other War Department Properties)
1911	Feb. 9	Lincoln Memorial, District of Columbia (dedicated 1922)
1913	Oct. 14	Cabrillo NM, California (also listed with Other War Department Properties)
1916	July 17	Abraham Lincoln NP, Kentucky (also listed with Other War Department Properties)
1925	March 23	Mount Rushmore N MEM, South Dakota
1927	March 2	Kill Devil Hill Monument, North Carolina (redesignated Wright Brothers N MEM 1953; also listed with Other War Department Properties)
1928	May 23	George Rogers Clark Memorial, Indiana (incorporated in George Rogers Clark NHP 1966)
1932	May 21	Theodore Roosevelt Island, District of Columbia

National Battlefield Areas, 1890–1933

1890	Aug. 19	Chickamauga and Chattanooga NMP, Georgia and Tennessee
	Aug. 30	Antietam NBS, Maryland (redesignated a NB 1978)
1894	Dec. 27	Shiloh NMP, Tennessee
1895	Feb. 11	Gettysburg NMP, Pennsylvania
1899	Feb. 21	Vicksburg NMP, Mississippi
1907	March 4	Chalmette Monument and Grounds, Louisiana (redesignated Chalmette NHP 1939; incorporated in Jean Lafitte NHP & PRES 1978)
1917	Feb. 8	Kennesaw Mountain NBS, Georgia (redesignated a NBP 1935)
	March 2	Guilford Courthouse NMP, North Carolina
1926	June 2	Moores Creek NMP, North Carolina (redesignated a NB 1980)
	July 3	Petersburg NMP, Virginia (redesignated a NB 1962)
1927	Feb. 14	Fredericksburg and Spotsylvania County Battlefields Memorial NMP, Virginia
	March 3	Stones River NMP, Tennessee (redesignated a NB 1980)
1928	March 26	Fort Donelson NMP, Tennessee (redesignated a NB 1985)
1929	Feb. 21	Brices Cross Roads NBS, Mississippi
	Feb. 21	Tupelo NBS, Mississippi (redesignated a NB 1961)
	March 4	Cowpens NBS, South Carolina (redesignated a NB 1972)
1930	June 18	Appomattox Battlefield Site, Virginia (designated Appomattox Court House National Historical Monument 1935; redesignated a NHP 1954)
1931	March 4	Fort Necessity NBS, Pennsylvania (redesignated a NB 1961)
	March 4	Kings Mountain NMP, South Carolina

Other War Department Properties, 1910–1933

1910	June 23	Big Hole Battlefield NM, Montana (redesignated Big Hole NB 1963)
1913	Oct. 14	Cabrillo NM, California (also listed with National Memorials)

1916	July 17	Abraham Lincoln NP, Kentucky (redesignated a NHP 1939; redesignated Abraham Lincoln Birthplace NHS 1959; also listed with National Memorials)
1923	March 2	Mound City Group NM, Ohio (incorporated in Hopewell Culture NHP 1992)
1924	Oct. 15	Castle Pinckney NM, South Carolina (abolished 1956)
	Oct. 15	Fort Marion NM, Florida (redesignated Castillo de San Marcos NM 1942)
	Oct. 15	Fort Matanzas NM, Florida
	Oct. 15	Fort Pulaski NM, Georgia
	Oct. 15	Statue of Liberty NM, New York (also listed with National Memorials)
1925	Feb. 6	Meriwether Lewis NM, Tennessee (incorporated in Natchez Trace Parkway 1961)
	March 3	Fort McHenry NP, Maryland (redesignated Fort McHenry NM and Historic Shrine 1939)
	March 4	Lee Mansion, Virginia (date restoration authorized; designated Custis-Lee Mansion 1955; redesignated Arlington House, The Robert E. Lee Memorial, 1972)
	Sept. 5	Father Millet Cross NM, New York (abolished 1949)
1927	March 2	Kill Devil Hill Monument, North Carolina (also listed with National Memorials)
1930	May 29	Fort Washington Park, Maryland (transfer from War Dept. authorized)

Agriculture Department National Monuments, 1907–1933

1907	May 6	Cinder Cone NM, California (incorporated in Lassen Volcanic NP 1916)
	May 6	Lassen Peak NM, California (incorporated in Lassen Volcanic NP 1916)
	Nov. 16	Gila Cliff Dwellings NM, New Mexico
	Dec. 19	Tonto NM, Arizona
1908	Jan. 11	Grand Canyon NM, Arizona (incorporated in Grand Canyon NP 1919)
	Jan. 16	Pinnacles NM, California (transferred to Interior Dept. 1910)
	Feb. 7	Jewel Cave NM, South Dakota
	Dec. 7	Wheeler NM, Colorado (abolished 1950)
1909	March 2	Mount Olympus NM, Washington (incorporated in Olympic NP 1938)
	July 12	Oregon Caves NM, Oregon
1911	July 6	Devils Postpile NM, California

1915	Nov. 30	Walnut Canyon NM, Arizona
1916	Feb. 11	Bandelier NM, New Mexico (transferred to Interior Dept. 1932)
	Oct. 25	Old Kasaan NM, Alaska (abolished 1955)
1922	Jan. 24	Lehman Caves NM, Nevada (incorporated in Great Basin NP 1986)
	Oct. 14	Timpanogos Cave NM, Utah
1923	June 8	Bryce Canyon NM, Utah (redesignated Utah NP and transferred to Interior Dept. 1924; redesignated Bryce Canyon NP 1928)
1924	April 18	Chiricahua NM, Arizona
1929	May 11	Holy Cross NM, Colorado (abolished 1950)
1930	May 26	Sunset Crater NM, Arizona (redesignated Sunset Crater Volcano NM 1990)
1933	March 1	Saguaro NM, Arizona (redesignated a NP 1994)

IHS   International Historic Site
NB   National Battlefield
NBP   National Battlefield Park
NBS   National Battlefield Site
NHP   National Historical Park
NHP & PRES   National Historical Park and Preserve
NH RES   National Historical Reserve
NHS   National Historic Site
NL   National Lakeshore

NM   National Monument
NM & PRES   National Monument and Preserve
N MEM   National Memorial
NMP   National Military Park
NP   National Park
NP & PRES   National Park and Preserve
N PRES   National Preserve
NR   National River
NRA   National Recreation Area

NRRA   National River and Recreation Area
N RES   National Reserve
NS   National Seashore
NSR   National Scenic River/Riverway
NST   National Scenic Trail
PKWY   Parkway
SRR   Scenic and Recreational River
WR   Wild River
WSR   Wild and Scenic River

NPS Areas Resulting from the 1933 Reorganization

Abraham Lincoln Birthplace NHS, Kentucky
Antietam NB, Maryland
Appomattox Court House NHP, Virginia
Arlington House, The Robert E. Lee Memorial, Virginia
Big Hole NB, Montana
Brices Cross Roads NBS, Mississippi
Cabrillo NM, California
Castillo de San Marcos NM, Florida
Chickamauga and Chattanooga NMP, Georgia and Tennessee
Chiricahua NM, Arizona
Colonial NHP, Virginia—Yorktown National Cemetery
Cowpens NB, South Carolina
Devils Postpile NM, California
Ford's Theatre NHS, District of Columbia
Fort Donelson NB, Tennessee
Fort McHenry NM and Historic Shrine, Maryland
Fort Matanzas NM, Florida
Fort Necessity NB, Pennsylvania
Fort Pulaski NM, Georgia
Fredericksburg and Spotsylvania County Battlefields Memorial NMP, Virginia
George Washington Memorial PKWY, District of Columbia, Maryland, and Virginia
Gettysburg NMP, Pennsylvania
Gila Cliff Dwellings NM, New Mexico
Great Basin NP, Nevada—Lehman Caves portion
Guilford Courthouse NMP, North Carolina
Hopewell Culture NHP, Ohio—Mound City Group portion
Jean Lafitte NHP and Preserve, Louisiana—Chalmette unit
Jewel Cave NM, South Dakota
Kennesaw Mountain NBP, Georgia
Kings Mountain NMP, South Carolina
Lincoln Memorial, District of Columbia
Moores Creek NB, North Carolina
Natchez Trace PKWY, Mississippi—Meriwether Lewis Park
National Capital Parks, District of Columbia and Maryland
National Mall, District of Columbia

Olympic NP, Washington—Mount Olympus portion
Oregon Caves NM, Oregon
Petersburg NB, Virginia
Rock Creek Park, District of Columbia
Saguaro NP, Arizona
Shiloh NMP, Tennessee
Statue of Liberty NM, New York
Stones River NB, Tennessee
Sunset Crater Volcano NM, Arizona
Theodore Roosevelt Island, District of Columbia
Timpanogos Cave NM, Utah
Tonto NM, Arizona
Tupelo NB, Mississippi
Vicksburg NMP, Mississippi
Walnut Canyon NM, Arizona
Washington Monument, District of Columbia
White House, District of Columbia
Wright Brothers N MEM, North Carolina

IHS International Historic Site	**NM** National Monument	**NRRA** National River and Recreation Area
NB National Battlefield	**NM & PRES** National Monument and Preserve	**N RES** National Reserve
NBP National Battlefield Park		**NS** National Seashore
NBS National Battlefield Site	**N MEM** National Memorial	**NSR** National Scenic River/Riverway
NHP National Historical Park	**NMP** National Military Park	**NST** National Scenic Trail
NHP & PRES National Historical Park and Preserve	**NP** National Park	**PKWY** Parkway
	NP & PRES National Park and Preserve	**SRR** Scenic and Recreational River
NH RES National Historical Reserve	**N PRES** National Preserve	**WR** Wild River
NHS National Historic Site	**NR** National River	**WSR** Wild and Scenic River
NL National Lakeshore	**NRA** National Recreation Area	

Orville *(left)* and Wilbur Wright in 1904 on their Huffman Prairie, Ohio, test field. This photograph was taken the year following their first successful flight at Kitty Hawk.

From the New Deal to War and Peace, 1933 through 1951

Along with the great influx of parks from the reorganization, the National Park Service undertook another mission in 1933 as President Franklin D. Roosevelt launched his New Deal: helping to relieve the great economic depression then gripping the nation. Under NPS supervision, the new Civilian Conservation Corp (CCC) would employ thousands of jobless young men in a wide range of conservation, rehabilitation, and construction projects in both the national and state parks. At the program's peak in 1935 the NPS oversaw 600 CCC camps, 118 of them in national parklands and 482 in state parks, staffed by some 120,000 enrollees and 6,000 professional supervisors.

Besides its many park improvements, the CCC had lasting effects on NPS organization and personnel. Regional offices established to coordinate the CCC in the state parks evolved in 1937 into a permanent regional structure for management of the National Park System. Many of the landscape architects, engineers, foresters, biologists, historians, archeologists, and architects hired under the program's auspices remained on the rolls as career NPS employees.

The NPS had encouraged the state park movement ever since Stephen T. Mather had helped organize the National Conference on State Parks in 1921. State parks could protect deserving areas that did not meet national park standards and meet recreational needs beyond the proper scope of the NPS. Most states lacked any park system plans, prompting the NPS to advocate comprehensive new planning legislation as it became directly involved with state parks and recreational demonstration areas under the New Deal. The resulting Park, Parkway, and Recreation Area Study Act of 1936 enabled the NPS, working with others, to plan parkways and facilities at federal, state, and local levels throughout the country. Its first comprehensive report under the act, *A Study of the Park and Recreation Problem in the United States*, was published in 1941.

Horace Albright left the NPS for private business on August 9, 1933, just before the reorganization became effective. Secretary of the Interior Harold L. Ickes named Arno B. Cammerer, who had served as associate director, to succeed him. A competent if not dynamic director, Cammerer found life difficult under Roosevelt's irascible Secretary of Interior but remained in charge of the greatly expanded organization until 1940. Ickes then persuaded Newton B. Drury, a respected conservationist who had headed the Save-the-Redwoods League in California, to lead the NPS.

With America's entry into World War II in December 1941, Drury had to preside over a drastic retrenchment in NPS activity. The CCC program was dismantled, regular appropriations for the National Park System declined from $21 million in 1940 to $5 million in 1943, the number of full-time employees was slashed from 3,500 to fewer than 2,000, and public visits to the parks fell from 21 million in 1941 to 6 million in 1942. To free space in Washington for the war effort, unrelated government functions were exiled to other locations; NPS headquarters moved to the Merchandise Mart in Chicago and did not return until October 1947.

The war had other impacts on the System. Many of the National Capital Parks lands, including Potomac Park and the Washington Monument grounds, were covered with temporary office buildings and housing for the influx of war workers. Park hotels like the Ahwahnee at Yosemite were commandeered for the rest and rehabilitation of servicemen. The armed forces used Mount Rainier for mountain warfare training, Joshua Tree National Monument for desert training, and Mount McKinley for testing equipment under arctic conditions.

Some wartime pressures seriously threatened park resources. Timber interests sought to log Sitka spruce in Olympic National Park for airplane manufacture. Ranchers pushed to open many western areas for grazing. Mining companies wanted to search for copper at Grand Canyon and Mount Rainier, manganese at Shenandoah, and tungsten at Yosemite. Campaigners for scrap metal eyed historic cannon at the Service's battlefields and forts. Drury successfully fended off most such demands, yielding only in exceptional circumstances.

As America redirected its energies to domestic pursuits after the war, accelerated development of river basins by the Corps of Engineers and the Bureau of Reclamation posed a new round of threats

Civilian Conservation Corps enrollee, Beltsville, Maryland.
There were 600 CCC camps at national and state park areas during the 1930s.

to the System. The proposed Bridge Canyon Dam on the Colorado River would have impounded water through Grand Canyon National Monument into the adjacent national park; Glacier View Dam on the Flathead River in Montana threatened to flood 20,000 acres of Glacier National Park; the reservoir behind the proposed Mining City Dam on Kentucky's Green River would have periodically flooded the underground Echo River in Mammoth Cave; and dams on the Potomac above and below Great Falls would have submerged 40 miles of the historic Chesapeake and Ohio Canal. Bureau of Reclamation plans to flood wilderness canyons in Dinosaur National Monument with dams at Echo Park and Split Mountain on the Green River touched off a conservation battle recalling Hetch Hetchy. Secretary of the Interior Oscar L. Chapman's decision to support the project over NPS opposition contributed to Drury's forced resignation in March 1951. Congress later declined to approve the Dinosaur dams, however, and most other such proposals affecting parklands were dropped as well.

Arthur E. Demaray, long an NPS mainstay as associate director under Cammerer and Drury, became director for the eight months remaining before his retirement in December 1951. He was followed by Conrad L. Wirth, a landscape architect and planner who had led the Service's CCC program in the state parks. Wirth's major contribution as director, Mission 66, is touched on in the next chapter.

The Depression years saw no downturn in the growth of the National Park System. Expansion nearly ceased during the war but fully resumed thereafter. From the reorganization to 1951, 59 of today's units were added to the rolls. Forty of them were historical areas, increasing the numerical majority attained by this category in the reorganization. Eleven were predominantly natural in character, and eight would be classified as recreational.

Natural Areas

Two entirely new national parks, one national memorial park later redesignated a national park, and eight national monuments protecting natural features joined the System between August 1933 and 1951; and three essentially new national parks were formed or expanded from preexisting holdings. Seven of these national monuments were later converted to or incorporated in six national parks and a national seashore.

Everglades National Park in Florida was authorized in 1934 to protect the largest tropical wilderness in the United States. It was the only national park in the far southeastern states until 1980 and remains the only one of its kind. Congress authorized Big Bend

National Park a year later to encompass more than 700,000 acres of wilderness country in southwestern Texas, including the Chisos Mountains and three magnificent canyons in the great bend of the Rio Grande. Theodore Roosevelt National Memorial Park, established in 1947 and redesignated a national park in 1978, includes scenic badlands along the Little Missouri River and part of Roosevelt's Elkhorn Ranch in North Dakota.

During his first seven years in office Franklin Roosevelt routinely used the Antiquities Act to proclaim seven national monuments. Cedar Breaks protected a remarkable natural amphitheater of eroded limestone and sandstone in southwestern Utah; Joshua Tree preserved a characteristic part—initially 825,340 acres—of the Mojave and Colorado deserts in southern California; Organ Pipe Cactus incorporated 325,000 acres of the Sonoran Desert in southern Arizona; Capitol Reef preserved a 20-mile segment of the great Waterpocket Fold in south-central Utah; and Channel Islands protected Santa Barbara and Anacapa islands, the smallest in a group of eight off the coast of southern California. Joshua Tree, Capitol Reef, and Channel Islands later became national parks. A second Zion National Monument, proclaimed in 1937, was incorporated in the existing Zion National Park in 1956. Santa Rosa Island National Monument near Pensacola, Florida, was abolished only seven years after its proclamation in 1939, but the island returned to the System as part of Gulf Islands National Seashore in 1971.

Roosevelt's eighth national monument proclamation was far from routine. Its subject was Jackson Hole, Wyoming, discussed as a possible addition to Yellowstone National Park as early as 1892. John D. Rockefeller, Jr., visited the area in 1926 with Horace Albright, then superintendent of Yellowstone, and was disturbed to see commercial development on private lands despoiling the view of the Teton Range. With official encouragement and without publicly disclosing his role and purpose, Rockefeller undertook to purchase more than 33,000 acres through his Snake River Land Company for donation to the United States. When the scheme became public, cattlemen, hunters, timbermen, and other local interests bitterly opposed the land's removal from economic productivity, hunting, and taxation. Wyoming's congressional delegation came to their aid by thwarting passage of park enabling legislation. In response, Roosevelt in 1943 proclaimed Jackson Hole National Monument to accept Rockefeller's donation. The monument also included 179,000 acres from Teton National Forest adjoining the limited Grand Teton National Park established in 1929.

Roosevelt's proclamation produced a storm of criticism about Jackson Hole in particular and use of the Antiquities Act to circumvent Congress in general. Bills were introduced to abolish the monument and repeal the act's proclamation authority. Legislation abolishing the monument passed Congress in 1944 but was vetoed by Roosevelt; the proclamation was also contested unsuccessfully in court. Meanwhile, the monument's foes saw that Congress appropriated no money for its management. A legislative compromise was finally reached in 1950, when most of Jackson Hole National Monument and the old Grand Teton National Park were incorporated in a new Grand Teton National Park of some 298,000 acres. The act contained special provisions for tax revenue compensation and hunting in the park; it also prohibited establishing national monuments or enlarging national parks in Wyoming thereafter except by congressional action.

After the Jackson Hole controversy, Presidential proclamation of national monuments outside Wyoming nearly ceased as well. Only six more monuments were so established between 1943 and 1978. Two were natural features: Buck Island Reef in the Virgin Islands, ordered by President John F. Kennedy in 1961; and Marble Canyon, Arizona, proclaimed by President Lyndon B. Johnson on his last day in office in 1969 (and added to Grand Canyon National Park in 1975). The others were of mostly cultural significance: Effigy Mounds, Iowa, by President Harry S Truman in 1949; Edison Laboratory, New Jersey, and the Chesapeake and Ohio Canal in Maryland by President Dwight D. Eisenhower in 1956 and 1961; and Russell Cave, Alabama, by President Kennedy in 1961. President Jimmy Carter's 1978 proclamation of 11 monuments in Alaska, the most substantial use of the Antiquities Act to expand the National Park System, occurred under exceptional circumstances, to be discussed later. (Proclamation authority was not used again until 1996 when President William J. Clinton proclaimed Grand Staircase-Escalante National Monument in Utah but left it under the Bureau of Land Management. President Clinton later made extensive use of the proclamation authority to establish new national monuments and significantly expand others.)

Olympic and Kings Canyon were the other two essentially new national parks from 1933 to 1951 that encompassed existing holdings. Congress established Olympic National Park in Washington, incorporating Mount Olympus National Monument, in 1938 after an ardent campaign by park preservationists against timber interests. After a 50-year struggle involving power and irrigation proponents, lumbermen, ranchers, and hunters, Kings Canyon National Park came to fruition in 1940 to protect some 460,000 acres of mountain and canyon wilderness on the west slope of the Sierra Nevada. It incorporated and superseded General Grant, one of California's three original national parks of 1890.

Four previously authorized national parks were formally established during the period after sufficient lands were acquired from nonfederal sources: Great Smoky Mountains in 1934, Shenandoah in 1935, Isle Royale in 1940, and Mammoth Cave in 1941. President Roosevelt also used the Antiquities Act to order significant additions to several existing national monuments before the Jackson Hole proclamation controversy forced a moratorium on such actions. Death Valley was expanded by nearly 306,000 acres in 1937; 203,885 acres containing the spectacular wild canyons of the Yampa and Green rivers were added to Dinosaur in 1938; Glacier Bay received an additional 905,000 acres for wildlife and glacier protection in 1939; and 150,000 acres were added to Badlands that year.

Historical Areas

With the 1933 reorganization, historic preservation became a major responsibility of the National Park Service. Two years later Congress confirmed the Service's role as the leading federal agency in this field in the Historic Sites Act of August 21, 1935—the most significant general preservation enactment since the 1906 Antiquities Act.

The Historic Sites Act stemmed from desires within the NPS for stronger legal authority for its accelerated historical programs and from desires beyond the NPS for greater federal assistance to historic properties. It began by declaring "a national policy to preserve for public use historic sites, buildings and objects of national significance for the inspiration and benefit of the people of the United States."

To carry out this policy, the act assigned broad powers and duties to the Secretary of the Interior and the NPS. They were to survey historic properties "for the purpose of determining which possess exceptional value as commemorating or illustrating the history of the United States." They were authorized to conduct research; to restore, preserve, and maintain historic properties directly or through cooperative agreements with other parties; and to mark properties, establish and maintain related museums, and engage in other interpretive activities for public education. There was also a general authority for acquiring historic properties—provided that no federal funds were obligated in advance of congressional appropriations.

This restriction, from a House amendment to the draft bill prepared in the Interior Department, effectively curtailed the envisioned addition of properties to the National Park System by Secretarial action alone. The Secretary could designate "national historic sites" outside the System and accept their donation, but unless and until Congress provided funds for acquiring sites not donated and for administering those that were, the NPS could offer little more than moral support. Several additions up to 1951, including Salem Maritime in Massachusetts, Federal Hall and Vanderbilt Mansion in New York, and Hampton in Maryland, became national historic sites by Secretarial designation under the Historic Sites Act before being brought into the System by congressional action.

Although the act was of limited value by itself in enlarging the System, its provision for a historic sites survey—institutionalized within the NPS as the National Survey of Historic Sites and Buildings— proved valuable in identifying potential additions. Another product of the act, the Advisory Board on National Parks, Historic Sites, Buildings, and Monuments (retitled the National Park System Advisory Board in 1978), used outside experts in the cultural and natural resource disciplines to review selected properties and recommend those found nationally significant for Secretarial designation or inclusion in the System.

The first Secretarial designation under the Historic Sites Act was the Jefferson National Expansion Memorial in St. Louis on December 20, 1935. The designated area, fronting on the Mississippi River and encompassing 37 city blocks, was also the Service's first extensive urban responsibility outside Washington, D.C. Ironically, the designation served to justify federal expenditures for urban renewal and a modern memorial to western expansion rather than historic preservation. Most of the area was bulldozed, and the soaring Gateway Arch designed by Eero Saarinen was constructed as its centerpiece in the 1960s.

Salem Maritime National Historic Site was the first area so titled. Designated by Secretary Ickes on March 17, 1938, it included several important structures on Salem's waterfront dating from the city's maritime prominence in the 18th and 19th centuries. Hopewell Village, Pennsylvania, became the second national historic site on August 3, 1938. The CCC was put to work restoring portions of the site, a rural ironmaking plantation of the 19th century containing a blast furnace, ironmaster's mansion, and auxiliary structures. Its redesignation as Hopewell Furnace National Historic Site in 1985 reflected the historic name of the complex.

In 1948, responding to the recommendations of a study commission, Congress authorized another major historical project in an urban setting: Independence National Historical Park in Philadelphia. Among the most important historic districts in the United States, the park includes Independence Hall, Congress Hall, Carpenters Hall, and other features associated with the achievement of American independence and the establishment of government under the Constitution. In 1959 it was enlarged by incorporation of the old Philadelphia Custom House (Second Bank of the United States), which had been designated a national historic site 20 years before. In New York City, Federal Hall and Castle Clinton joined the Statue of Liberty under NPS administration.

Six United States Presidents were honored by additions to the System during the period, furthering a trend that would ultimately number Presidential sites second only to battlefields in the System's historical ranks. The Thomas Jefferson Memorial in Washington was authorized in 1934 and completed nine years later. Andrew Johnson's house and tailor shop in Greeneville, Tennessee, were acquired in 1935. Franklin D. Roosevelt's Hyde Park estate was designated a national historic site in 1944, while he was still President, and was donated after his death a year later. The residence of John Adams and his son John Quincy Adams in Quincy, Massachusetts, followed in 1946. As noted under natural areas, Theodore Roosevelt National Memorial Park was established in 1947.

The first new battlefield park to be authorized was Monocacy, scene of an 1864 Civil War engagement in Maryland; but the lands were not donated as expected, and Congress had to reauthorize their acquisition with appropriated funds in 1976 to make the park a reality. Civil War battlefield parks in Virginia at Richmond, authorized in 1936, and Manassas, designated in 1940, were more readily achieved. Congress authorized Saratoga National Historical Park, New York, in 1938 to commemorate the pivotal Revolutionary War battle there. As noted previously, the National Cemetery of Custer's Battlefield Reservation, Montana, was transferred from the War Department in 1940 and redesignated Custer Battlefield National Monument in 1946 and Little Bighorn Battlefield National Monument in 1991.

Fort Jefferson National Monument, Florida, containing the largest all-masonry fortification in the Western Hemisphere, was the first historical monument proclaimed by Franklin Roosevelt, in 1935. (Congress renamed it Dry Tortugas National Park in 1992.) Congress authorized Fort Stanwix National Monument, New York, in 1935; but the NPS did not acquire the site on which it would reconstruct the colonial and Revolutionary War fort until 1973. The second historical monument Roosevelt proclaimed was Fort Laramie, Wyoming, in 1938—the first of several western military and fur-trading posts to join the System. Fort Vancouver, Washington, followed by act of Congress in 1948. Fort Sumter, the famous Civil War landmark

Designed by Eero Saarinen and dedicated in 1968, 630-foot-high Gateway Arch is the focus of Jefferson National Expansion Memorial, St. Louis, Missouri.

53

at Charleston, South Carolina, was also transferred to the NPS that year by the Army.

Although sites representing political and military history predominated, a few areas representing other themes were admitted during the period. Two national historic sites representing commerce and industry—Salem Maritime and Hopewell Village—have been mentioned. The Chesapeake and Ohio Canal, running 185 miles from Washington, D.C., to Cumberland, Maryland, was acquired from the Baltimore and Ohio Railroad in 1938 as partial repayment of the railroad's government loans. This abandoned commercial waterway, built between 1828 and 1850, was proclaimed a national monument in 1961 and became the centerpiece of a national historical park a decade later. Harpers Ferry, West Virginia, famous for John Brown's raid and subsequent Civil War activity, was an important manufacturing center in the early 19th century. Congress authorized a national monument there in 1944 and an expanded national historical park in 1963. The first of several areas commemorating African Americans was George Washington Carver National Monument, authorized by Congress at the scientist-educator's Missouri birthplace just after his death in 1943.

Recreational Areas

Another new group of areas came under National Park Service administration during the 1933–51 period. Some were based on roads or reservoirs—modern developments rather than natural or historic resources. Others were based on natural resources that did not necessarily meet national park or monument standards and that were set aside primarily to be developed for intensive public use. Hunting and other activities traditionally barred from national parks might be permitted in these places. The reservoir-based areas were officially titled national recreation areas; the others were variously named but also came to be known collectively as recreational areas.

Among them were parkways—elongated parklands containing carefully designed and landscaped limited-access roads intended for recreational motoring rather than high-speed point-to-point travel. Parkways of this type originated in Westchester County, New York, during the second decade of the 20th century. Congress then authorized the Rock Creek and Potomac Parkway connecting Potomac Park with Rock Creek Park and the National Zoological Park in the District of Columbia, although this four-mile parkway—a component of National Capital Parks—was not completed until 1936. The next federal parkway was the Mount Vernon Memorial Highway of 1928–32. As mentioned previously, it was incorporated in the larger George

Washington Memorial Parkway, which the NPS acquired in the reorganization. During World War II the national capital parkway network was expanded with the authorization of Suitland Parkway, a landscaped access route to Andrews Air Force Base, Maryland, and the Baltimore-Washington Parkway, providing access to Fort Meade, Maryland. The NPS acquired responsibility for these parkways in 1949 and 1950 and later sought unsuccessfully to transfer them to Maryland. Since 1975 it has classed them as components of National Capital Parks rather than discrete National Park System units.

Colonial Parkway, providing a 23-mile scenic drive between Jamestown and Yorktown, Virginia, was the first federal parkway outside the national capital area. It was authorized in 1930 as part of Colonial National Monument and remains a component of the present national historical park. By far the greatest federal projects of this kind were the Blue Ridge and Natchez Trace parkways, authorized in 1933 and 1934. Rather than serving primarily local traffic, these protected recreational roads traverse long stretches of scenic and historic rural landscape. Both were begun as New Deal public works projects and soon became National Park System units.

Skyline Drive in Shenandoah National Park, personally promoted by President Hoover and begun as a Depression relief project under his administration in 1932, was the prototype for the Blue Ridge Parkway. After Franklin Roosevelt's inauguration, the National Industrial Recovery Act of June 16, 1933, authorized Secretary Ickes in his capacity as public works administrator to prepare a comprehensive public works program, including the "construction, repair, and improvement of public highways and park ways." Sen. Harry F. Byrd, Sr., of Virginia and others seized the opportunity to propose a scenic parkway linking Skyline Drive to Great Smoky Mountains National Park. Roosevelt and Ickes embraced the proposal, Virginia and North Carolina agreed to donate the right-of-way, and that December the NPS received an initial $4 million allotment for the project. Jointly planned by the NPS and the Bureau of Public Roads, it was named the Blue Ridge Parkway and legally assigned to NPS administration in 1936. The popular 470-mile parkway, completed over several decades, alternates sweeping views of the southern highlands with intimate glimpses of Appalachian flora and fauna and traditional log structures.

During the early 19th century the Natchez Trace from Nashville, Tennessee, to Natchez, Mississippi, became an important route binding

Visitors at the Purgatory Mountain overlook, mile 92.2 on the Blue Ridge Parkway in Virginia, 1940s.

the Old Southwest to the rest of the country. Congress authorized a survey for a Natchez Trace Parkway along the historic route in 1934 and gave the NPS responsibility for its development and administration in 1938. Nearly all of the projected 444 miles of road have now been completed, linking such features as Mount Locust, the earliest surviving inn on the trace, and Emerald Mound, one of the largest prehistoric ceremonial structures in the United States.

Proposals for other parkways proliferated during the 1930s, and many were revived after the war. Among them were an Appalachian Parkway continuing Skyline Drive to Maine and a southern extension of the Blue Ridge Parkway to Georgia; a Mississippi River Parkway; a southern extension of the George Washington Memorial Parkway to Wakefield (Washington's birthplace) and Williamsburg; a parkway from Washington to Gettysburg; and a Chesapeake and Ohio Canal Parkway along and atop the historic waterway.

These proposals had much appeal in the era before other well-engineered limited-access highways eased long-distance travel, but they also stirred opposition. The Wilderness Society was organized in 1935 partly to protest such ridgecrest roadways as the Skyline Drive and Blue Ridge Parkway, criticized as intrusions in the natural environment. In 1954 William O. Douglas, U.S. Supreme Court justice and wilderness advocate, led a highly publicized week-long hike along the C&O Canal to fight the Service's parkway plan there, effectively killing it. Such stands by conservationists, the interstate highway program, and economic considerations virtually halted new parkway construction by the mid-1960s.

The National Industrial Recovery Act also authorized federal purchase of lands considered submarginal for farming but suitable for recreation. After acquisition by the Federal Emergency Relief Administration, they were transferred to the Resettlement Administration and then to the NPS for recreational demonstration projects. By 1936 the NPS had set up 46 projects encompassing 397,000 acres in 24 states.

From the beginning it was intended that most of the recreational demonstration areas would be turned over to state and local governments, and in 1942 Congress provided the necessary authority. By 1946 the NPS had largely completed the conveyances but retained portions of several areas. Most of the retained lands were added to existing System units, including Acadia and Shenandoah national parks, White Sands National Monument in New Mexico, and Hopewell Village National Historic Site. Theodore Roosevelt National Memorial Park incorporated two recreational demonstration areas when established in 1947. Three recreational demonstration areas became discrete units of the System: Secretary Ickes used the Historic Sites Act to designate Bull Run Recreational Demonstration Area and additional donated land in Virginia as Manassas National Battlefield Park in 1940; Chopawamsic Recreational Demonstration Area, Virginia, became Prince William Forest Park in 1948; and part of Catoctin Recreational Demonstration Area in Maryland became Catoctin Mountain Park in 1954. The latter surrounds the Presidential retreat inaugurated by President Franklin D. Roosevelt as Shangri-La and renamed Camp David by President Dwight D. Eisenhower. Prince William Forest and Catoctin Mountain parks were originally treated as outlying components of National Capital Parks; the NPS did not count them as discrete System units until 1968.

Greenbelt Park, Maryland, like Catoctin Mountain and Prince William Forest parks, lacks "national" status. The Public Housing Authority transferred it to the NPS in 1950 when the NPS acquired the adjoining Baltimore-Washington Parkway from the Bureau of Public Roads. Initially carried as part of National Capital Parks, the suburban park offers camping for visitors to the Washington area and other recreational facilities for nearby residents. Despite its purely local significance, the NPS began listing it as a separate System unit in 1975.

As noted above, fierce conservation battles were fought during the period against dams that threatened to inundate unspoiled canyons in and near certain national parks and monuments. There was some displeasure, then, when the NPS joined forces with the dam builders to administer recreational developments and activities at major impoundments. The first of these involvements came at Lake Mead in Nevada and Arizona, created by Hoover Dam. The Bureau of Reclamation completed the dam, then called Boulder Dam, on the Colorado River in 1935. The next year, under an agreement with Reclamation, the NPS assumed responsibility for all recreational activities on its reservoir at what was first titled Boulder Dam Recreation Area.

The responsibility became a major one, for Lake Mead at capacity is 115 miles long with 550 miles of shoreline, affording extensive opportunities for boating, swimming, and camping. By 1952 Davis Dam had been built downstream, impounding the 67-mile-long Lake Mohave, and the NPS acquired similar duties there. The total Lake Mead National Recreation Area, as it was renamed in 1947, covers both lakes and surrounding lands totaling nearly 1,500,000 acres, making it the largest as well as the first area with this designation in the National Park System.

The second permanent unit of this kind, Coulee Dam National Recreation Area in Washington, was established in 1946 under another agreement with the Bureau of Reclamation patterned after that for Lake Mead. The Grand Coulee Dam, completed in 1941, created Franklin D. Roosevelt Lake—151 miles long with a 660-mile shoreline. The NPS developed campgrounds, marinas, bathing facilities, and other amenities at some three dozen locations in what was redesignated Lake Roosevelt National Recreation Area in 1997.

The Service's other major recreational initiative during the period addressed seashores. In 1934 it surveyed the Atlantic and Gulf coasts and identified 12 significant areas deserving federal protection.

Glen Canyon Dam with Lake Powell in background. Below the dam, the Colorado River cuts through the Grand Canyon.

Among them was Cape Hatteras, North Carolina, which Congress authorized as the first national seashore in 1937. Land acquisition lagged until after World War II; the Mellon family foundations then made substantial grants to help North Carolina purchase and donate the needed lands. The seashore encompasses almost 100 miles of barrier islands and beaches, providing an outstanding natural resource base for surf bathing, sport fishing, nature study, and other recreational activities.

1933	June 16	Blue Ridge PKWY, North Carolina and Virginia (acquired 1936)
	Aug. 22	Cedar Breaks NM, Utah
1934	May 30	Everglades NP, Florida
	June 14	Ocmulgee NM, Georgia
	June 19	Natchez Trace PKWY, Mississippi, Alabama, and Tennessee (acquired 1938)
	June 21	Monocacy NMP, Maryland (reauthorized and redesignated a NB 1976)
	June 26	Thomas Jefferson Memorial, District of Columbia (dedicated 1943)
1935	Jan. 4	Fort Jefferson NM, Florida (redesignated Dry Tortugas NP 1992)
	June 20	Big Bend NP, Texas
	Aug. 21	*Historic Sites Act*
	Aug. 21	Fort Stanwix NM, New York (acquired 1973)
	Aug. 27	Ackia Battleground NM, Mississippi (incorporated in Natchez Trace PKWY 1961)
	Aug. 29	Andrew Johnson NM, Tennessee (redesignated a NHS 1963)
	Dec. 20	Jefferson National Expansion Memorial, Missouri (Gateway Arch authorized 1954, dedicated 1968)
1936	March 2	Richmond NBP, Virginia
	March 19	Homestead NM of America, Nebraska
	May 26	Fort Frederica NM, Georgia
	June 2	Perry's Victory and International Peace Memorial NM, Ohio (redesignated Perry's Victory and International Peace Memorial 1972)
	June 23	*Park, Parkway, and Recreation Area Study Act*
	June 29	Whitman NM, Washington (redesignated Whitman Mission NHS 1963)
	Aug. 16	Joshua Tree NM, California (incorporated in Joshua Tree NP 1994)
	Oct. 13	Boulder Dam Recreation Area, Nevada and Arizona (redesignated Lake Mead NRA 1947)
	Nov. 14	Bull Run Recreational Demonstration Area, Virginia (redesignated Manassas NBP 1940)
	Nov. 14	Catoctin Recreational Demonstration Area, Maryland (redesignated Catoctin Mountain Park 1954)
	Nov. 14	Chopawamsic Recreational Demonstration Area, Virginia (redesignated Prince William Forest Park 1948)
1937	Jan. 22	Zion NM, Utah (incorporated in Zion NP 1956)
	April 13	Organ Pipe Cactus NM, Arizona
	Aug. 2	Capitol Reef NM, Utah (redesignated a NP 1971)
	Aug. 17	Cape Hatteras NS, North Carolina
	Aug. 25	Pipestone NM, Minnesota
1938	March 17	Salem Maritime NHS, Massachusetts

1938	April 26	Channel Islands NM, California (incorporated in Channel Islands NP 1980)
	June 1	Saratoga NHP, New York
	June 29	Olympic NP, Washington (incorporated Mount Olympus NM)
	July 16	Fort Laramie NM, Wyoming (redesignated a NHS 1960)
	Aug. 3	Hopewell Village NHS, Pennsylvania (redesignated Hopewell Furnace NHS 1985)
	Sept. 23	Chesapeake and Ohio Canal, District of Columbia, Maryland, and West Virginia (date acquired; designated a NM 1961; incorporated in Chesapeake and Ohio Canal NHP 1971)
1939	May 17	Santa Rosa Island NM, Florida (abolished 1946; island included in Gulf Islands NS 1971)
	May 26	Federal Hall Memorial NHS, New York (redesignated Federal Hall N MEM 1955)
	May 26	Philadelphia Custom House NHS, Pennsylvania (incorporated in Independence NHP 1959)
	July 1	Mount Rushmore N MEM, South Dakota (date acquired)
	July 25	Tuzigoot NM, Arizona
1940	March 4	Kings Canyon NP, California (incorporated General Grant NP)
	June 11	Cumberland Gap NHP, Kentucky, Virginia, and Tennessee
	July 1	National Cemetery of Custer's Battlefield Reservation, Montana (date acquired; redesignated Custer Battlefield NM 1946; redesignated Little Bighorn Battlefield NM 1991)
	Aug. 12	Fort Washington Park, Maryland
	Dec. 18	Vanderbilt Mansion NHS, New York
1941	April 5	Fort Raleigh NHS, North Carolina
1943	March 15	Jackson Hole NM, Wyoming (incorporated in Grand Teton NP 1950)
	July 14	George Washington Carver NM, Missouri
1944	Jan. 15	Home of Franklin D. Roosevelt NHS, New York
	June 30	Harpers Ferry NM, Maryland and West Virginia (redesignated a NHP 1963)
	Oct. 13	Atlanta Campaign NHS, Georgia (abolished 1950)
1945	May 22	Millerton Lake Recreation Area, California (abolished 1957)
	May 22	Shasta Lake Recreation Area, California (transferred to Forest Service 1948)
1946	April 18	Lake Texoma Recreation Area, Oklahoma and Texas (transferred to Corps of Engineers 1949)
	Aug. 12	Castle Clinton NM, New York
	Dec. 9	Adams Mansion NHS, Massachusetts (redesignated Adams NHS 1952; redesignated Adams NHP 1998)
	Dec. 18	Coulee Dam NRA, Washington (redesignated Lake Roosevelt NRA 1997)

1947	April 25	Theodore Roosevelt National Memorial Park, North Dakota (redesignated a NP 1978)
1948	March 11	DeSoto N MEM, Florida
	April 28	Fort Sumter NM, South Carolina
	June 19	Fort Vancouver NM, Washington (redesignated a NHS 1961)
	June 22	Hampton NHS, Maryland
	June 28	Independence NHP, Pennsylvania (incorporated Independence Hall NHS, designated 1943)
1949	Feb. 14	San Juan NHS, Puerto Rico
	June 8	Saint Croix Island NM, Maine (redesignated an International Historic Site 1984)
	Aug. 17	Suitland PKWY, District of Columbia and Maryland (date acquired; incorporated in National Capital Parks 1975)
	Oct. 25	Effigy Mounds NM, Iowa
1950	Aug. 3	Baltimore-Washington PKWY, Maryland (date acquired; incorporated in National Capital Parks 1975)
	Aug. 3	Greenbelt Park, Maryland
	Sept. 14	Grand Teton NP, Wyoming (incorporated 1929 NP and Jackson Hole NM)
	Sept. 21	Fort Caroline N MEM, Florida

IHS	International Historic Site	NM	National Monument	NRRA	National River and Recreation Area
NB	National Battlefield	NM & PRES	National Monument and Preserve	N RES	National Reserve
NBP	National Battlefield Park	N MEM	National Memorial	NS	National Seashore
NBS	National Battlefield Site	NMP	National Military Park	NSR	National Scenic River/Riverway
NHP	National Historical Park	NP	National Park	NST	National Scenic Trail
NHP & PRES	National Historical Park and Preserve	NP & PRES	National Park and Preserve	PKWY	Parkway
NH RES	National Historical Reserve	N PRES	National Preserve	SRR	Scenic and Recreational River
NHS	National Historic Site	NR	National River	WR	Wild River
NL	National Lakeshore	NRA	National Recreation Area	WSR	Wild and Scenic River

Rococo-style furnishings at Vanderbilt Mansion National Historic Site were typical of Gilded Age opulence in the 1890s.

Mission 66 and the Environmental Era, 1952 through 1972

When Conrad L. Wirth took over as National Park Service director in December 1951, he inherited a National Park System besieged by its admiring public. Increasing personal incomes, leisure time, and automobile ownership fueled a postwar travel boom for families young and old, and the national parks, it seemed, bore the brunt of it. Visits to the parks mounted from the six million of 1942 to 33 million in 1950 en route to 72 million in 1960. With few improvements since the CCC era and park appropriations again cut during the Korean War, obsolete and deteriorating park roads, campgrounds, employee housing, sanitary systems, and other facilities were overwhelmed.

Wirth's response was Mission 66, a 10-year program to upgrade facilities, staffing, and resource management throughout the System by the 50th anniversary of the NPS in 1966. President Dwight D. Eisenhower endorsed the program after Wirth gave a slide presentation of park conditions at a January 1956 Cabinet meeting. Congress proved equally receptive, appropriating more than a billion dollars over the 10-year period for Mission 66 improvements. Dozens of park visitor centers, hundreds of employee residences, and the Mather and Albright employee training centers at Harpers Ferry and the Grand Canyon are among the program's enduring legacies.

Mission 66 resurrected an array of other activities that the NPS had foregone during its lean years, including resumption of the National Survey of Historic Sites and Buildings to aid in planning for the System's orderly expansion. Beginning in 1960 most historic properties surveyed and found nationally significant were designated national historic landmarks by Secretaries of the Interior. In 1962 the NPS launched a similar program for natural lands, resulting in the designation of national natural landmarks. Although these programs continued to help identify areas meriting inclusion in the System, their larger function was to officially recognize outstanding places not proposed as parks and encourage their preservation by others. By 1999 some 2,300 historic properties and nearly 600 natural areas had received landmark designation.

George B. Hartzog Jr. succeeded Wirth in January 1964. A hard-driving lawyer and administrator, Hartzog had made his mark as superintendent of the Jefferson National Expansion Memorial, where he laid the foundation for the Gateway Arch. Stewart L. Udall, Interior Secretary under Presidents John F. Kennedy and Lyndon B. Johnson, found Hartzog a willing ally in advancing an activist park policy for Johnson's Great Society. During Hartzog's nine-year tenure, 68 of today's park units were added—nearly three-quarters as many as had been added in the preceding 30 years. There were new kinds of parks—rivers, trails, performance facilities, urban recreation areas—and new directions for NPS managers and professionals.

Management of natural resources within the System underwent changes following a 1963 report by a committee of distinguished scientists chaired by A. Starker Leopold. "As a primary goal, we would recommend that the biotic associations within each park be maintained, or where necessary recreated, as nearly as possible in the condition that prevailed when the area was first visited by the white man," the Leopold Report declared. "A national park should represent a vignette of primitive America." The natural roles of predators, once routinely killed, and wildfire, customarily suppressed, received special attention.

In the field of interpretation, "living history" programs ranging from military demonstrations to farming became popular attractions at many areas. Environmental interpretation, emphasizing ecological relationships, and special environmental education programs for school classes reflected and promoted the nation's growing environmental awareness.

The Service's historic preservation activities expanded further beyond the parks. Responding to the destructive effects of urban renewal, highway construction, and other federal projects during the postwar era, the National Historic Preservation Act of 1966 authorized the NPS to maintain a comprehensive National Register of Historic Places. National Register properties—locally significant places as well as national historic landmarks in both public and private ownership—would receive special consideration in federal project planning and various forms of preservation assistance.

National Park Service Director Conrad L. Wirth at the dedication of the Death Valley park visitor center, 1960.

On July 10, 1964, Secretary Udall signed a management policy memorandum prepared by Hartzog and his staff. "In looking back at the legislative enactments that have shaped the National Park System, it is clear that the Congress has included within the growing System three different categories of areas—natural, historical, and recreational," it said.

"Each of these categories requires a separate management concept and a separate set of management principles coordinated to form one organic management plan for the entire System." Natural areas were to be managed for perpetuation and restoration of their natural values, although significant historic features present should be maintained "to the extent compatible with the primary purpose for which the area was established." In historical areas these emphases were reversed. In recreational areas, natural and historic resource preservation would be subordinate to public use; the primary objective was to foster "active participation in outdoor recreation in a pleasing environment."

Previously, a 1953 act of Congress had legally defined the National Park System to exclude most areas in the recreational category. That law had reflected concern that if reservoirs, hunting, and other such developments and uses were allowed anywhere in the System, they might spread to the more traditional areas as well. Udall's memorandum seemingly violated the 1953 act by granting System membership to all recreational areas, but it allayed the underlying concern by placing them in a subclass with distinct management policies. The NPS developed separate policy manuals for the three area categories and published them in 1968. Two years later law caught up with administrative initiative: the General Authorities Act of August 18, 1970, redefined the System to include all areas managed "for park, monument, historic, parkway, recreational, or other purposes" by the NPS.

Udall's memorandum also called for continued expansion of the System "through inclusion of additional areas of scenic, scientific, historical and recreational value to the Nation." This perennial objective was reiterated in another policy memorandum signed June 18, 1969, by President Richard Nixon's first Interior Secretary, Walter J. Hickel. "The National Park System should protect and exhibit the best examples of our great national landscapes, riverscapes and shores and undersea environments; the processes which formed them; the life communities that grow and dwell therein; and the important landmarks of our history," it said. "There are serious gaps and inadequacies which must be remedied while opportunities still exist if the System is to fulfill the people's need always to see and understand their heritage of history and the natural world.

"You should continue your studies to identify gaps in the System and recommend to me areas that would fill them. It is my hope that we can make a significant contribution to rounding out more of the National Park System in these next few years." With this charge in hand, Hartzog ordered preparation of a National Park System Plan, published in 1972. Its history component divided American history into thematic categories like those used in national historic landmark studies. Historical parks were assigned to the categories, revealing gaps wherever the categories were unrepresented. By maximizing the number of categories and allowing each park to represent only one of them, the plan determined that at least 196 new parks were needed to treat all major aspects of American history. The plan's natural history component similarly identified more than 300 aspects of natural history requiring initial or greater representation.

Although recreational areas did not lend themselves to the same kind of thematic analysis and were not addressed in the plan, they now composed the fastest growing category of parks. Of the 98 permanent additions to the System from 1952 through 1972, 28 fell in the recreational category—more than triple the number added during the 1933–51 period. Historical additions continued to lead, totaling 58. Only 12 additions were classed as natural. This modest increase in traditional national parks and natural monuments reflected the reduced availability of lands meeting traditional natural park standards and capable of management under traditional park policies. In fact, however, many of the recreational areas were as much natural in character as recreational in use.

Additions in all categories were aided by the Land and Water Conservation Fund Act of 1965. As amended in 1968, the act earmarked revenues from visitor fees, surplus property sales, motorboat fuel taxes, and offshore oil and gas leasing for federal and state parkland acquisition. The fund was administered by the Bureau of Outdoor Recreation, a new Interior Department bureau established in 1962 on the recommendation of the Outdoor Recreation Resources Review Commission, chaired by Laurance S. Rockefeller. Wirth opposed creation of the new bureau, which took away the Service's responsibilities for recreation planning and assistance along with some of its staff and funds. Ultimately the NPS regained these functions when BOR, reconstituted in 1978 as the Heritage Conservation and Recreation Service, expired in 1981.

Natural Areas

Of the 12 permanent additions in the natural area category, seven were national parks and five were national monuments. A thirteenth addition, Marble Canyon National Monument, was later incorporated in Grand Canyon National Park.

Congress authorized Virgin Islands National Park, the first natural addition of the period, in 1956 to protect nearly two-thirds of the land mass and most of the colorful offshore waters of St. John Island. The park owes its existence to the contributions of Laurance Rockefeller's Jackson Hole Preserve, Inc. Buck Island Reef, also in the Virgin Islands, was the first natural monument of the period in 1961. In Hawaii, the crater of 10,023-foot Haleakalā on the island of Maui was taken from Hawaii National Park in 1960 and placed in a separate Haleakalā National Park. The parent park was retitled Hawai'i Volcanoes in 1961. This division of a national park remains unique.

Canyonlands National Park was established in 1964 to protect a remote region of exceptional scenic quality and archeological and scientific importance at the confluence of the Green and Colorado rivers in southeastern Utah. A 1971 addition brought the park's total area to more than 337,000 acres.

Congress authorized Guadalupe Mountains National Park in 1966 to preserve an area in West Texas "possessing outstanding geological values together with scenic and other natural values of great significance." Proposed for inclusion in the System as early as 1933, the park's mountain mass and adjoining lands cover more than 86,000 acres and include portions of the world's most extensive Permian limestone fossil reef.

North Cascades National Park in the state of Washington embraces nearly 505,000 acres of wild alpine country with jagged peaks, mountain lakes, and glaciers. The park proposal was surrounded by intense controversy involving timber and mining interests, conservationists, local governments, the Forest Service, and the Bureau of Outdoor Recreation as well as the NPS. Congress finally authorized the park in 1968 simultaneously with Redwood National Park, California.

Redwood, which also came into being after long and bitter controversy, was intended "to preserve significant examples of the primeval coastal redwood forests and the streams and seashores with which they are associated for purposes of public inspiration, enjoyment and scientific study." Within its legislated boundaries, enlarged in 1978 to encompass 110,000 acres, are three jointly managed state parks dating from the 1920s, 40 miles of Pacific coastline, and the world's tallest trees.

Redwood's establishment and enlargement entailed the taking of valuable private timberlands and compensatory benefits to affected loggers. It was by far the most expensive park ever, costing some $1.5 billion for land acquisition alone.

The last new national park of the period was Voyageurs, on Minnesota's northern border, authorized in 1971 to preserve the "scenery, geological conditions, and waterway system which constituted a part of the historic route of the Voyageurs who contributed significantly to the opening of the Northwest United States." It occupies 218,000 acres of remote northern lake country.

Besides the seven new national parks, Arches and Capitol Reef national monuments in Utah were redesignated national parks by legislation in 1971, and a new national monument, Biscayne in the upper Florida keys, formed the basis for Biscayne National Park in 1980. Congress authorized three other new monuments—Agate Fossil Beds, Nebraska; Florissant Fossil Beds, Colorado; and Fossil Butte, Wyoming—to protect outstanding deposits of mammal, insect, and fish fossils.

Of much importance to natural preservation in the System during and after this period was the Wilderness Act of September 3, 1964. "In order to assure that an increasing population, accompanied by expanding settlement and growing mechanization, does not occupy and modify all areas within the United States and its possessions, leaving no lands designated for preservation and protection in their natural condition, it is hereby declared to be the policy of the Congress to secure for the American people of present and future generations the benefits of an enduring resource of wilderness," the act declared. "For this purpose there is hereby established a National Wilderness Preservation System to be composed of federally owned areas designated by Congress as 'wilderness areas', and these shall be administered for the use and enjoyment of the American people in such manner as will leave them unimpaired for future use and enjoyment as wilderness. . . ."

The act defined wilderness as "an area where the earth and its community of life are untrammeled by man, where man himself is a visitor who does not remain." For designation as wilderness an area was to be without permanent improvements or human habitation, to retain its "primeval character and influence," and generally to contain at least 5,000 acres. Among other provisions, the act directed the Secretary of the Interior to review within 10 years all roadless areas of 5,000 acres or more in the National Park System and to report to the President on their suitability for wilderness designation. The President was then to report his recommendations to Congress for action.

Wirth had opposed application of the wilderness legislation to the System, believing that the NPS recognized and managed wilderness sufficiently without it. Because Congress declined to exempt the System, the act forced a careful examination of all potentially qualifying parklands and consideration as to which should be perpetuated without roads, use of motorized equipment, structures, or other developments incompatible with formal wilderness designation. By 2005 the NPS had studied many potential wilderness areas, and Congress had confirmed more than half of NPS lands as wilderness.

Historical Areas

Sixty-one historical areas joined the System from the beginning of 1952 to the end of 1972. Three of them—St. Thomas and Mar-A-Lago national historic sites and the National Visitor Center—were later dropped, leaving 58 still present.

Twelve of the additions—more than a fifth of the permanent total—were Presidential sites. The Theodore Roosevelt Association donated Roosevelt's New York City birthplace and Sagamore Hill, his estate at Oyster Bay, New York, in 1962. In 1966 the Ansley Wilcox house at Buffalo, New York, where Roosevelt became President after William McKinley's assassination, was added to the System, becoming known as Theodore Roosevelt Inaugural National Historic Site. (The Roosevelt memorial on Theodore Roosevelt Island in Washington, D.C., was dedicated a year later.) Another Abraham Lincoln site, Lincoln Boyhood National Memorial, was accepted from the state of Indiana in 1962, and Lincoln's residence in Springfield, Illinois, became Lincoln Home National Historic Site a decade later. This fifth and most illustrative Lincoln site tied him with Theodore Roosevelt as the most commemorated President in the System.

Ulysses S. Grant's Tomb in New York City became General Grant National Memorial in 1958. The following year Congress authorized the Franklin Delano Roosevelt Memorial in Washington, D.C., although it was not completed and dedicated until 1997. A national historic site was established at Herbert Hoover's birthplace and grave in West Branch, Iowa, in 1965, a year after his death. In 1967 Dwight D. Eisenhower saw his farm at Gettysburg, Pennsylvania, designated a national historic site, and John F. Kennedy was posthumously honored by a national historic site at his Brookline, Massachusetts, birthplace. William Howard Taft National Historic Site, containing the 27th President's Cincinnati birthplace and boyhood residence, and Lyndon B. Johnson National Historic Site, ultimately comprising Johnson's birthplace, boyhood house, grandfather's ranch, and LBJ Ranch in Blanco and Gillespie counties, Texas, were authorized together in 1969.

Even more sites addressed military history. Representing the Civil War were Pea Ridge National Military Park, Arkansas, Wilson's Creek National Battlefield, Missouri, and Andersonville National Historic

Site, Georgia, where the notorious prison camp was located. Horseshoe Bend National Military Park, Alabama, preserved the site where Gen. Andrew Jackson defeated the Creeks in 1814, and Minute Man National Historical Park included the first battlegrounds of the American Revolution in Lexington and Concord, Massachusetts. There were more frontier forts, including Fort Union, New Mexico; Bent's Old Fort, Colorado; Fort Davis, Texas; Fort Smith, Arkansas; Fort Bowie, Arizona; Fort Larned, Kansas; and Fort Union Trading Post in North Dakota and Montana. Fort Point National Historic Site encompassed a mid-19th-century San Francisco harbor defense. An unassuming Philadelphia boardinghouse became Thaddeus Kosciuszko National Memorial in 1972 to honor the Polish military engineer who served in the American Revolution and briefly occupied the property later.

Other themes were increasingly represented as well. Christiansted National Historic Site preserved structures associated with Danish colonization of the Virgin Islands. Edison National Historic Site comprised the inventor's last laboratory and residence at West Orange, New Jersey. Golden Spike National Historic Site marked the joining of the first transcontinental railroad in 1869 at Promontory Summit, Utah; Allegheny Portage Railroad National Historic Site contained the remains of an earlier mechanical conveyance over the mountains in Pennsylvania. Saugus Iron Works National Historic Site encompassed a reconstructed 17th-century industrial complex near Boston. Another facet of economic and social history was addressed by Grant-Kohrs Ranch National Historic Site, Montana, containing one of the largest post-Civil War open range ranches in the country.

The residences of three literary figures—Henry Wadsworth Longfellow, John Muir, and Carl Sandburg—became national historic sites, as did the house and studio of the sculptor Augustus Saint-Gaudens. Congress authorized a national memorial for Roger Williams, founder of Rhode Island and a pioneer in religious freedom. Chamizal National Memorial in El Paso, Texas, commemorated the peaceful settlement of a 99-year boundary dispute with Mexico. The System recognized two more noted African Americans at Booker T. Washington National Monument in Virginia and the Frederick Douglass Home, later a national historic site, in Washington, D.C.

Two other historical additions in the national capital region warrant mention. Congress authorized Piscataway Park in 1961 to pre-

Presidents Theodore Roosevelt and Abraham Lincoln—shown here on Mount Rushmore National Memorial—are the most commemorated individuals in the National Park System.

serve the natural quality of the Potomac riverbank opposite Mount Vernon, largely through the acquisition of scenic easements. It is the only System unit existing primarily for scenic protection of another property. Chesapeake and Ohio Canal National Historical Park, authorized by Congress in 1971, incorporates the former national monument and significant additional land on the north bank of the Potomac between Great Falls and Cumberland, Maryland. Thus buffered, the canal combines natural, historical, and recreational values to a degree unsurpassed by any other single resource in the System.

With enactment of the National Historic Preservation Act of 1966, all historical parks were entered in the National Register of Historic Places. This made NPS and other federal agency actions affecting them subject to review by state historic preservation officers and the Advisory Council on Historic Preservation, a new federal agency established by the act.

A 1971 Presidential order required the NPS to nominate to the National Register all qualifying historic features in its natural and recreational areas as well. These resources, most of local or regional significance, were now entitled to the same consideration as the historical parks when faced with potentially harmful actions. The increased attention to historic resources outside parks categorized as historical tended to blur the distinctions among the area categories, contributing to the Service's decision to terminate their official status in 1977.

Recreational Areas
As noted above, 28 permanent additions to the National Park System from 1952 through 1972 fell in the recreational category. More than half were seashores and reservoir-related areas along with another parkway. The others were new kinds of areas: lakeshores, rivers, a performing arts facility, a trail, and two major urban recreation complexes.

In 1963 the recently formed Recreation Advisory Council, composed of six Cabinet-level officials, proposed a system of national recreation areas and set criteria for them. They were to be spacious, generally including at least 20,000 acres of land and water. They were to be within 250 miles of urban centers and accommodate heavy, multi-state patronage.

Their natural endowments would need to be "well above the ordinary in quality and recreation appeal, being of lesser significance than the unique scenic and historic elements of the National Park System, but affording a quality of recreation experience which transcends that normally associated with areas provided by State and local governments." The scale of investment and development was to be high enough to warrant federal involvement. Cooperative management arrangements involving the Forest Service, the Corps of Engineers, and possibly other federal bureaus besides the NPS were expected.

The recreational area category formally adopted by the NPS in 1964 reflected the Recreation Advisory Council's criteria, although not all units that the NPS assigned to the category were of the type envisioned by the council. Several areas were categorized as recreational largely by default, because they did not fully meet the Service's criteria and policies for natural or historical areas.

The NPS resumed shoreline studies in the mid-1950s with generous support from the Mellon family foundations. Their results were published in *Our Vanishing Shoreline* (1955), *A Report on the Seashore Recreation Survey of the Atlantic and Gulf Coasts* (1955), *Our Fourth Shore: Great Lakes Shoreline Recreation Area Survey* (1959), and *Pacific Coast Recreation Area Survey* (1959). The NPS also prepared detailed studies of individual projects. The fruits of this program included eight more national seashores and four national lakeshores during the period. Most of them forestalled residential, commercial, and highway development and protected natural and historic features.

Cape Cod National Seashore, Massachusetts, authorized in 1961, protects the dunes and marshes of Cape Cod's lower arm along a 40-mile strip. It was the first large natural or recreational area for which Congress at the outset allowed money to be appropriated for land acquisition. Another novel provision of the Cape Cod legislation prevented the Secretary of the Interior from condemning private improved property once local jurisdictions had implemented zoning regulations meeting his approval.

This "Cape Cod formula," designed to avert serious conflicts between the government and local communities and stabilize the landscape without forced resettlement of numerous families, was an important precedent for legislation authorizing other such additions to the System. A third innovation in the Cape Cod act, also adopted elsewhere, was the establishment of a park advisory commission representing the state and affected local jurisdictions.

Point Reyes and Padre Island national seashores followed two weeks apart in 1962, extending the Service's seashore holdings to the Pacific and Gulf coasts. Point Reyes incorporates more than 40 miles

The California coast's signature fog envelopes the lighthouse at Point Reyes National Seashore.

of Pacific shoreline north of San Francisco, including Drakes Bay and Tomales Point. Padre Island National Seashore covers 80 miles of the long Texas barrier island on the Gulf of Mexico. Fire Island National Seashore, authorized in 1964, protects some 25 miles of barrier beach on Long Island's south shore 50 miles from Manhattan. Congress distanced Fire Island from the recreational area concept by ordering the Secretary of the Interior to administer it "with the primary aim of conserving the natural resources located there."

Assateague Island National Seashore, authorized in 1965, occupies a 35-mile-long barrier island on the Eastern Shore of Maryland and Virginia within reach of the Baltimore and Washington metropolitan areas. Political compromises resulted in joint management by the NPS, U.S. Fish and Wildlife Service, and Maryland's Department of Forests and Parks. The seashore legislation directed the NPS to build a highway and major concession developments along the island, but growing awareness of barrier island dynamics and opposition by environmentalists led Congress to repeal these requirements in 1976.

The 1966 act authorizing Cape Lookout National Seashore, extending southwest from Cape Hatteras National Seashore on North Carolina's Outer Banks, also subordinated natural conservation to recreation. Like Assateague, however, Cape Lookout has been lightly developed for recreational use.

Gulf Islands National Seashore, authorized in 1971, came closer than its predecessors to the Recreation Advisory Council's vision of a national recreation area. The offshore islands in its Mississippi portion nevertheless contain natural and historic features whose preservation is of first importance, and a Spanish fort within its boundaries near Pensacola, Florida, is a national historic landmark.

The final national seashore of the period, Cumberland Island, Georgia, was least consistent with the recreational area concept. Its 1972 legislation included stringent development restrictions: with certain exceptions, "the seashore shall be permanently preserved in its primitive state, and no development of the project or plan for the convenience of visitors shall be undertaken which would be incompatible with the preservation of the unique flora and fauna . . . , nor shall any road or causeway connecting Cumberland Island to the mainland be constructed." It remains among the most "natural" of the seashores.

The four national lakeshores, authorized in 1966 and 1970, generally followed the seashore pattern. Indiana Dunes, on the southern shore of Lake Michigan between Gary and Michigan City, Indiana, had been proposed as a national park as early as 1917. Although it was the most urban of the four, serving the greater Chicago area, its legislation stressed natural conservation at least as much as it did recreation.

Sleeping Bear Dunes, Michigan, occupying 34 miles of shoreline on upper Lake Michigan, was to be managed "in a manner which provides for recreational opportunities consistent with the maximum protection of the natural environment within the area." Pictured Rocks, Michigan, the first of the national lakeshores, and Apostle Islands, Wisconsin, both on Lake Superior, also protect resources of great natural and scenic value. Had the laws authorizing most of the seashores and lakeshores not permitted hunting, many would have readily fitted the Service's natural area category.

The NPS became involved at 12 existing or proposed reservoirs during the 1952–72 period. Ten of these national recreation areas are still in the System, two having been transferred to Forest Service administration. As with their predecessors, NPS responsibilities were set by cooperative agreements, although several were authorized by specific acts of Congress. Four deserve special mention.

Glen Canyon National Recreation Area, inaugurated in 1958, encompasses Lake Powell, formed by Glen Canyon Dam on the Colorado River in northern Arizona and extending into southeastern Utah. The 186-mile-long impoundment was the price conservationists paid for their defeat of the Echo Park Dam in Dinosaur National Monument earlier that decade. An arm of the reservoir provides boat access to Rainbow Bridge National Monument, formerly remote and difficult to reach.

Congress authorized Ross Lake and Lake Chelan national recreation areas, Washington, together with the adjacent North Cascades National Park in 1968. They were planned as areas in which to concentrate visitor accommodations and other development outside the national park—the first time such an arrangement was made in conjunction with initial park legislation. The Ross Lake area lies between the north and south units of the national park, which Lake Chelan adjoins on the southeast.

Delaware Water Gap National Recreation Area in Pennsylvania and New Jersey was authorized in 1965 to include the proposed Tocks Island Reservoir and scenic lands in the Delaware Valley totaling 71,000 acres. The System's first national recreation area east of the Mississippi was envisioned to serve 10 million visitors annually from the New York and Philadelphia metropolitan areas. But the Tocks Island Dam came under heavy attack from environmentalists and others, especially after the National Environmental Policy Act of 1969 forced greater consideration of the environmental effects of such projects. Without repealing the authorization for the dam,

Congress in 1978 ordered the Corps of Engineers to transfer lands acquired for the reservoir to the NPS and made the Delaware River within the recreation area a national scenic river—a designation incompatible with its damming. No other National Park System unit differs more from its original concept.

The first of the national rivers and scenic riverways was Ozark National Scenic Riverways in Missouri, authorized by Congress in 1964 "for the purpose of conserving and interpreting unique scenic and other natural values and objects of historic interest, including preservation of portions of the Jacks Fork River in Missouri as free-flowing streams, preservation of springs and caves, management of wildlife, and provisions for use and enjoyment of the outdoor recreation resources thereof. . . ." This linear area incorporates some 140 miles of river and three state parks in its 80,790 acres.

The Ozark authorization foreshadowed the comprehensive Wild and Scenic Rivers Act of October 2, 1968. The act "declared to be the policy of the United States that certain selected rivers of the Nation, which, with their immediate environments, possess outstandingly remarkable scenic, recreational, geologic, fish and wildlife, historic, cultural, or other similar values, shall be preserved in free-flowing condition, and that they and their immediate environments shall be protected for the benefit and enjoyment of present and future generations." The act identified eight rivers and adjacent lands in nine states as initial components of a national wild and scenic rivers system, to be administered variously by the Secretaries of Agriculture and the Interior. Only one of them, Saint Croix National Scenic Riverway in Minnesota and Wisconsin, became a unit of the National Park System. Ideal for canoeing, it contains some 230 miles of the Saint Croix River, and its Namekagon tributary is noted for clear flowing water and abundant wildlife.

The act named 27 other rivers or river segments to be studied as potential additions to the wild and scenic rivers system. All or parts of the study areas later joined the System: 27 more miles of the Saint Croix were authorized for Saint Croix National Scenic Riverway in 1972, Obed Wild and Scenic River in Tennessee was authorized in 1976, and Rio Grande Wild and Scenic River and Upper Delaware Scenic and Recreational River followed in 1978. In 1972 Congress also authorized a similar addition not proposed in the Wild and Scenic Rivers Act—Buffalo National River, Arkansas. Its 94,309 acres encompass 136 miles of the Buffalo River, multicolored bluffs, and numerous springs.

On the same day that President Johnson approved the Wild and Scenic Rivers Act, North Cascades and Redwood national parks, and

Lake Chelan and Ross Lake national recreation areas, he also signed the National Trails System Act. The act provided for national recreation trails accessible to urban areas, to be designated by the Secretary of the Interior or the Secretary of Agriculture according to specified criteria; and national scenic trails, generally longer and more remote, to be established by Congress. It designated two national scenic trails as initial components of the trails system: the Appalachian Trail, extending 2,100 miles from Mount Katahdin, Maine, to Springer Mountain, Georgia; and the Pacific Crest Trail, running 2,600 miles from Canada to Mexico along the Cascades, Sierras, and other ranges.

The Pacific Crest Trail would be administered by the Secretary of Agriculture and the Appalachian Trail by the Secretary of the Interior. The Appalachian Trail was thus brought into the National Park System. Conceived in 1921 by Benton MacKaye, forester and philosopher, it was largely completed by 1937. With its inclusion in the System, the NPS became responsible for its protection and maintenance within federally administered areas; states were encouraged to care for other portions. An advisory council appointed by the Secretary of the Interior under the act includes representatives of the 14 states through which the trail passes, the Appalachian Trail Conference, other private organizations, and involved federal agencies.

The National Trails System Act ordered 14 other routes to be studied for possible national scenic trail designation. Four of them later received the designation, two becoming units of the System in 1983: Natchez Trace National Scenic Trail, paralleling the Natchez Trace Parkway; and Potomac Heritage National Scenic Trail, running from the mouth of the Potomac River to Conemaugh Gorge in Pennsylvania, partly along the C&O Canal towpath. Congress designated five more as national scenic trails and 14 more as national historic trails between 1978 and 2003; the NPS gained coordinating roles for many of them, but not administrative responsibilities sufficient to list them as National Park System units.

Congress authorized the last of the four parkways now classed as System units in 1972. The John D. Rockefeller, Jr. Memorial Parkway is an 82-mile scenic corridor linking West Thumb in Yellowstone and the northern boundary of Grand Teton National Park. The only national parkway west of the Mississippi, it commemorates Rockefeller's generous contributions to several parks, including Grand Teton.

The NPS became involved with another new kind of park in 1966, when department store heiress Catherine Filene Shouse donated part of her Wolf Trap Farm in Fairfax County, Virginia, to the United States for a performing arts center. The Filene Center, an open-sided auditorium, was completed for its first summer season in 1971. Performances at Wolf Trap National Park for the Performing Arts are arranged by the private Wolf Trap Foundation. The NPS also had custody of the John F. Kennedy Center for the Performing Arts in Washington, D.C., from 1972 until 1994, when Congress gave its board of trustees full responsibility for it.

Performing arts assumed major roles at two other park units during the period, Chamizal National Memorial in El Paso, Texas, and Ford's Theatre National Historic Site in Washington, D.C. To further its theme of international amity, Chamizal accommodates performing groups from Mexico and the United States. The NPS restored Ford's Theatre, which it had acquired in the 1933 reorganization and maintained as the Lincoln Museum, as an operating theater in 1965-68. Because both places had historical commemoration and interpretation as their primary purposes, they were classed as historical rather than recreational areas.

On October 27, 1972, President Nixon approved the last two additions of the Hartzog years. Gateway National Recreation Area in New York City and nearby New Jersey and Golden Gate National Recreation Area in San Francisco and Marin County, California, may also have been the most consequential innovations of the period. Each contained seacoast beaches, but their locations and inclusion of other elements made them far more urban in character and patronage than the national seashores.

Gateway encompasses four major units totaling more than 26,500 acres. In Jamaica Bay, the primary aim is conservation of bird life and other natural resources. At Breezy Point, Staten Island, and Sandy

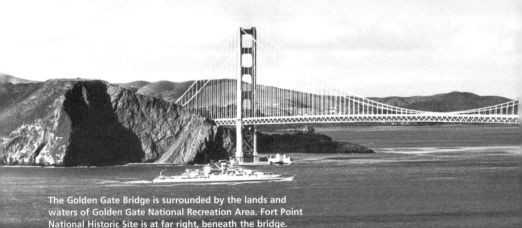

The Golden Gate Bridge is surrounded by the lands and waters of Golden Gate National Recreation Area. Fort Point National Historic Site is at far right, beneath the bridge.

Hook, recreational beach use predominates, although the legislation made special provision for preserving and using the historic structures on Sandy Hook and Staten Island. The Secretary of the Interior designated Sandy Hook's Fort Hancock and the Sandy Hook Proving Grounds a national historic landmark in 1982.

Golden Gate was established "to preserve for public use and enjoyment certain areas . . . possessing outstanding natural, historic, scenic, and recreational values, and in order to provide for the maintenance of needed recreational open space necessary to urban environment and planning." As at Gateway, much came from decommissioned military installations.

Within Golden Gate's more than 75,000 acres are restored native habitat, a coastal redwood forest, historic coastal defenses, Alcatraz, and the Presidio of San Francisco, transferred from the Army in 1994. A maritime museum and historic ship collection originally part of the national recreation area was spun off as San Francisco Maritime National Historical Park in 1988.

Before Gateway and Golden Gate, nearly all the Service's holdings in major urban areas outside the national capital region had been small historic sites, where the primary concerns were historic preservation and interpretation. These two acquisitions placed the NPS squarely in the business of urban mass recreation for essentially local populations—not previously a federal responsibility. Like earlier departures into historic sites, parkways, and reservoir areas, this move stirred controversy about the bureau's proper role. Attendant burdens of funding, staffing, and management refocus would prove significant challenges for years to come.

1952	March 4	Virgin Islands NHS, Virgin Islands (redesignated Christiansted NHS 1961)
	June 27	Shadow Mountain Recreation Area, Colorado (transferred to Forest Service 1979)
	July 9	Coronado N MEM, Arizona
1954	June 28	Fort Union NM, New Mexico
1955	July 26	City of Refuge NHP, Hawaii (redesignated Pu'uhonua o Hōnaunau NHP 1978)
	Dec. 6	Edison Home NHS, New Jersey (incorporated in Edison NHS 1962)
1956	April 2	Booker T. Washington NM, Virginia
	July 14	Edison Laboratory NM, New Jersey (incorporated in Edison NHS 1962)
	July 20	Pea Ridge NMP, Arkansas
	July 25	Horseshoe Bend NMP, Alabama
	Aug. 2	Virgin Islands NP, Virgin Islands
1958	April 18	Glen Canyon NRA, Utah and Arizona
	May 29	Fort Clatsop N MEM, Oregon (incorporated in Lewis and Clark NHP 2004)
	Aug. 14	General Grant N MEM, New York
	Sept. 2	Grand Portage NM, Minnesota (designated a NHS 1951)
1959	April 14	Minute Man NHS, Massachusetts (redesignated a NHP Sept. 21)
	Sept. 1	Franklin Delano Roosevelt Memorial, District of Columbia (dedicated 1997)
1960	April 22	Wilson's Creek Battlefield NP, Missouri (redesignated Wilson's Creek NB 1970)
	June 3	Bent's Old Fort NHS, Colorado
	July 6	Arkansas Post N MEM, Arkansas
	Sept. 13	Haleakalā NP, Hawaii (detached from Hawaii NP)
	Dec. 24	St. Thomas NHS, Virgin Islands (abolished 1975)
1961	May 11	Russell Cave NM, Alabama
	Aug. 7	Cape Cod NS, Massachusetts
	Sept. 8	Fort Davis NHS, Texas
	Sept. 13	Fort Smith NHS, Arkansas
	Oct. 4	Piscataway Park, Maryland
	Dec. 28	Buck Island Reef NM, Virgin Islands
1962	Feb. 19	Lincoln Boyhood N MEM, Indiana
	April 27	Hamilton Grange N MEM, New York
	May 31	Whiskeytown-Shasta-Trinity NRA, California (Whiskeytown Unit)
	July 25	Sagamore Hill NHS, New York
	July 25	Theodore Roosevelt Birthplace NHS, New York

1962	Sept. 5	Edison NHS, New Jersey (incorporated Edison Home NHS and Edison Laboratory NM)
	Sept. 5	Frederick Douglass Home, District of Columbia (redesignated Frederick Douglass NHS 1988)
	Sept. 13	Point Reyes NS, California
	Sept. 28	Padre Island NS, Texas
1963	July 22	Flaming Gorge Recreation Area, Utah and Wyoming (transferred to Forest Service 1968)
1964	Aug. 27	Ozark National Scenic Riverways, Missouri
	Aug. 30	Fort Bowie NHS, Arizona
	Aug. 31	Allegheny Portage Railroad NHS, Pennsylvania
	Aug. 31	Fort Larned NHS, Kansas
	Aug. 31	John Muir NHS, California
	Aug. 31	Johnstown Flood N MEM, Pennsylvania
	Aug. 31	Saint-Gaudens NHS, New Hampshire
	Sept. 3	*Land and Water Conservation Fund Act*
	Sept. 3	*National Wilderness Preservation System Act*
	Sept. 11	Fire Island NS, New York
	Sept. 12	Canyonlands NP, Utah
	Dec. 31	Bighorn Canyon NRA, Wyoming and Montana
1965	Feb. 1	Arbuckle NRA, Oklahoma (incorporated in Chickasaw NRA 1976)
	Feb. 11	Curecanti NRA, Colorado
	March 15	Sanford NRA, Texas (redesignated Lake Meredith Recreation Area 1972; redesignated Lake Meredith NRA 1990)
	May 15	Nez Perce NHP, Idaho
	June 5	Agate Fossil Beds NM, Nebraska
	June 28	Pecos NM, New Mexico (incorporated in Pecos NHP 1990)
	July 30	Golden Spike NHS, Utah (designated 1957)
	Aug. 12	Herbert Hoover NHS, Iowa
	Aug. 28	Hubbell Trading Post NHS, Arizona
	Aug. 31	Alibates Flint Quarries and Texas Panhandle Pueblo Culture NM, Texas (redesignated Alibates Flint Quarries NM 1978)
	Sept. 1	Delaware Water Gap NRA, Pennsylvania and New Jersey
	Sept. 21	Assateague Island NS, Maryland and Virginia
	Oct. 22	Roger Williams N MEM, Rhode Island
	Nov. 11	Amistad Recreation Area, Texas (redesignated Amistad NRA 1990)
1966	March 10	Cape Lookout NS, North Carolina
	June 20	Fort Union Trading Post NHS, Montana and North Dakota
	June 30	Chamizal N MEM, Texas
	July 23	George Rogers Clark NHP, Indiana
	Sept. 9	San Juan Island NHP, Washington
	Oct. 15	*National Historic Preservation Act*
	Oct. 15	Guadalupe Mountains NP, Texas
	Oct. 15	Pictured Rocks NL, Michigan

1966	Oct. 15	Wolf Trap Farm Park for the Performing Arts, Virginia (redesignated Wolf Trap National Park for the Performing Arts 2002)
	Nov. 2	Theodore Roosevelt Inaugural NHS, New York
	Nov. 5	Indiana Dunes NL, Indiana
1967	May 26	John Fitzgerald Kennedy NHS, Massachusetts
	Nov. 27	Eisenhower NHS, Pennsylvania
1968	March 12	National Visitor Center, District of Columbia (abolished 1981)
	April 5	Saugus Iron Works NHS, Massachusetts
	Oct. 2	*National Trails System Act*
	Oct. 2	*National Wild and Scenic Rivers System Act*
	Oct. 2	Appalachian NST, Maine, New Hampshire, Vermont, Massachusetts, Connecticut, New York, New Jersey, Pennsylvania, Maryland, West Virginia, Virginia, Tennessee, North Carolina, Georgia
	Oct. 2	Lake Chelan NRA, Washington
	Oct. 2	North Cascades NP, Washington
	Oct. 2	Redwood NP, California
	Oct. 2	Ross Lake NRA, Washington
	Oct. 2	Saint Croix NSR, Minnesota and Wisconsin
	Oct. 17	Carl Sandburg Home NHS, North Carolina
	Oct. 18	Biscayne NM, Florida (incorporated in Biscayne NP 1980)
1969	Jan. 20	Marble Canyon NM, Arizona (incorporated in Grand Canyon NP 1975)
	Aug. 20	Florissant Fossil Beds NM, Colorado
	Dec. 2	Lyndon B. Johnson NHS, Texas (redesignated a NHP 1980)
	Dec. 2	William Howard Taft NHS, Ohio
1970	Aug. 18	*General Authorities Act*
	Sept. 26	Apostle Islands NL, Wisconsin
	Oct. 16	Andersonville NHS, Georgia
	Oct. 16	Fort Point NHS, California
	Oct. 21	Sleeping Bear Dunes NL, Michigan
1971	Jan. 8	Chesapeake and Ohio Canal NHP, District of Columbia, Maryland, and West Virginia (incorporated Chesapeake and Ohio Canal NM)
	Jan. 8	Gulf Islands NS, Florida and Mississippi
	Jan. 8	Voyageurs NP, Minnesota
	Aug. 18	Lincoln Home NHS, Illinois
	Dec. 18	*Alaska Native Claims Settlement Act*
1972	March 1	Buffalo NR, Arkansas
	June 16	John F. Kennedy Center for the Performing Arts, District of Columbia (date acquired; transferred to Kennedy Center Trustees 1994)
	Aug. 17	Pu'ukoholā Heiau NHS, Hawaii
	Aug. 25	Grant-Kohrs Ranch NHS, Montana

1972	Aug. 25	John D. Rockefeller, Jr. Memorial PKWY, Wyoming
	Oct. 9	Longfellow NHS, Massachusetts
	Oct. 21	Hohokam Pima NM, Arizona
	Oct. 21	Mar-A-Lago NHS, Florida (designated 1969; abolished 1980)
	Oct. 21	Thaddeus Kosciuszko N MEM, Pennsylvania
	Oct. 23	Cumberland Island NS, Georgia
	Oct. 23	Fossil Butte NM, Wyoming
	Oct. 27	Gateway NRA, New York and New Jersey
	Oct. 27	Golden Gate NRA, California

IHS International Historic Site
NB National Battlefield
NBP National Battlefield Park
NBS National Battlefield Site
NHP National Historical Park
NHP & PRES National Historical Park and Preserve
NH RES National Historical Reserve
NHS National Historic Site
NL National Lakeshore

NM National Monument
NM & PRES National Monument and Preserve
N MEM National Memorial
NMP National Military Park
NP National Park
NP & PRES National Park and Preserve
N PRES National Preserve
NR National River
NRA National Recreation Area

NRRA National River and Recreation Area
N RES National Reserve
NS National Seashore
NSR National Scenic River/Riverway
NST National Scenic Trail
PKWY Parkway
SRR Scenic and Recreational River
WR Wild River
WSR Wild and Scenic River

Rounding Out the System, 1973 through 2004

In the final period of this account, expansion of the National Park System outpaced the explosive growth of the preceding period, despite a marked slowdown during most of President Ronald Reagan's administration. One hundred thirty-one new or essentially new parks were created from 1973 through 2004. This number does not tell the full story, for as a result of huge additions in Alaska in 1978 and 1980, the System's total land area more than doubled.

In January 1973 President Nixon replaced George Hartzog with Ronald H. Walker, a former White House assistant. Lacking previous park experience, Walker selected Russell E. Dickenson, a career park ranger and manager who had lately headed the National Capital Parks, as deputy director. Walker and Dickenson sought to consolidate past gains rather than expand the System at the previous rate, believing that NPS funding and staffing would be insufficient to sustain such continued growth.

Departing from recent stands, the NPS and Interior Department, backed by the Advisory Board on National Parks, opposed proposals for two more big urban recreation areas: Cuyahoga Valley between the Ohio cities of Akron and Cleveland, and Santa Monica Mountains near Los Angeles. Gateway and Golden Gate had been intended as models for state and local recreation areas elsewhere, they contended, not as prototypes for future units of the National Park System serving local populations.

The attempt to apply the brakes had little apparent effect. Congress authorized 14 more parks during Walker's two years as director. Six were small historic sites assembled in an omnibus bill. But they also included a major historical park in Boston, the first two national preserves, the controversial Cuyahoga Valley National Recreation Area, and another national seashore.

Walker's political base evaporated with Nixon's resignation in August 1974, and he left at the beginning of 1975. Secretary of the Interior Rogers C. B. Morton again looked to the career ranks of the NPS for Walker's successor, Gary Everhardt, who had joined the bureau as an engineer in 1957 and risen to the superintendency of Grand Teton National Park in 1972. In Everhardt's first year as director the NPS tightened its criteria for national parklands. Previously, to qualify for recommendation an area had to be nationally significant and lend itself to administration, preservation, and public use. Now the bureau would also consider whether the area was assured of adequate protection outside the System and whether it would be available for public appreciation and use under such protection. If so, the NPS would be unlikely to favor its acquisition.

A majority in Congress still favored expansion, however. Section 8 of the General Authorities Act of October 7, 1976, ordered specific measures to that end: "The Secretary of the Interior is directed to investigate, study, and continually monitor the welfare of areas whose resources exhibit qualities of national significance and which may have potential for inclusion in the National Park System. At the beginning of each fiscal year, the Secretary shall transmit to the [Congress] comprehensive reports on each of those areas upon which studies have been completed. On this same date . . . the Secretary shall transmit a listing . . . of not less than twelve such areas which appear to be of national significance and which may have potential for inclusion in the National Park System." A 1980 amendment to Section 8 also required submission of an updated National Park System plan "from which candidate areas can be identified and selected to constitute units of the National Park System."

In July 1977 Cecil D. Andrus, President Jimmy Carter's Interior Secretary, replaced Everhardt with William J. Whalen, who had worked in the National Capital Parks and as superintendent of Golden Gate National Recreation Area. Whalen's background and backing by Rep. Phillip Burton of California, the powerful chairman of the House subcommittee on parks, inclined him to favor urban parks and the many other new area proposals advanced by Burton and his colleagues. Burton's expansionism was epitomized by another omnibus enactment, the National Parks and Recreation Act of November 10, 1978. Characterized by critics as "park barrel" legislation, it authorized 15 additions to the System. Among them, despite another opposing resolution by the advisory board, was Santa Monica Moun-

The contribution of steam-powered rail transportation to the development of the United States is celebrated at Steamtown National Historic Site in Scranton, Pennsylvania.

tains National Recreation Area in California. Three weeks later, by different means, came the influx of Alaska parklands.

Friction with park concessioners in 1980 prompted Andrus to return Whalen to Golden Gate that May, and Russell Dickenson, who had directed the Service's Pacific Northwest Region since December 1975, came back to Washington in the top job. His less expansive posture would soon win greater favor: when President Reagan's first Interior Secretary, James G. Watt, took office in January 1981, he fully supported Dickenson's view that the NPS should improve its stewardship of what it had before seeking more.

Consistent with this approach, the 97th Congress (1981–82) eliminated appropriations for the new area studies dictated by Section 8, acquiesced in Dickenson's decision to shelve the expansionist National Park System plan, and declined to authorize a single new park. Instead, it and the next Congress supported the Service's Park Restoration and Improvement Program, which devoted more that a billion dollars over five years to stabilize and upgrade existing park resources and facilities.

In 1978 the Carter administration had reassigned the Service's programs of recognizing and assisting natural and cultural properties outside the System to the Heritage Conservation and Recreation Service (HCRS), an administrative reconstitution of the Bureau of Outdoor Recreation (BOR). The new Interior bureau, combining such activities as the National Register of Historic Places, the natural and historic landmarks programs, and the Land and Water Conservation Fund, did not function smoothly. Secretary Watt, a previous director of BOR, promptly abolished HCRS and returned all its functions to the NPS in 1981.

Dickenson's nearly five-year tenure restored stability to the NPS after its frequent turnover in leadership during the 1970s. The moratorium on new parks also helped the bureau catch its breath. There was only one concrete addition from the beginning of 1981 to Dickenson's retirement in March 1985 and for more than a year thereafter: Harry S Truman National Historic Site, Missouri. Two national scenic trails were authorized but advanced little beyond the planning stage. Dickenson's successor in May 1985 was William Penn Mott, Jr., an NPS landscape architect and planner in the 1930s and head of the California state park system under Gov. Ronald Reagan from 1967 to 1975. Deeply interested in interpretation, Mott sought a greater NPS role in educating the public about American history and environmental values. He also returned the NPS to a more expansionist posture, supporting the addition of Steamtown National Historic Site, Pennsylvania, and Great Basin National Park, Nevada, in

1986, Jimmy Carter National Historic Site in Georgia and El Malpais National Monument in New Mexico in 1987, and a dozen more areas in 1988.

Mott remained for nearly four years to April 1989, when James M. Ridenour became director under President George H.W. Bush. Ridenour had overseen Indiana's state park system as head of that state's Department of Natural Resources. As NPS director he took a more conservative attitude toward expansion than his predecessor, declaring that additions of less-than-national significance were "thinning the blood" of the National Park System. He urged alternatives to full federal acquisition of proposed parklands and stressed the importance of working with public and private partners to protect valuable lands in and outside the System. In 1990 Ridenour collaborated with Secretary of the Interior Manuel Lujan Jr. on a historic battlefield protection initiative and witnessed the largest single donation for parks ever: $10.5 million from the Richard King Mellon Foundation for needed lands at Antietam, Gettysburg, Fredericksburg, and Petersburg battlefields, Pecos National Historical Park, and Shenandoah National Park. Ridenour departed with the George H. W. Bush administration in January 1993, and Roger G. Kennedy came aboard under President William J. Clinton that June. Formerly director of the Smithsonian Institution's National Museum of American History, Kennedy had spoken and written extensively on historical topics. He reemphasized the need for partnerships to further NPS objectives and sought a greater educational role for the bureau beyond the parks, through such media as the internet.

Kennedy resigned in March 1997, and that August Robert G. Stanton became the fifteenth director of the National Park Service. The first NPS careerist in the post since Dickenson, he had been a park superintendent, an assistant director, and regional director of the Service's National Capital Region. Under legislation enacted in 1996, he was the first appointee to the position required to undergo Senate confirmation—not a problem given the good relations he had long maintained with Congress. He was also the Service's first African American director.

Republicans took control of Congress midway through President Clinton's first term, and with support from the Democratic former chairman of the House parks subcommittee they advanced legislation directing a reassessment of the criteria and procedures for adding areas to the System and a reevaluation of existing parks. Although the National Park System Reform Act would have led at most to recommendations for removing some areas from the System, requiring further congressional action for actual divestiture, Secretary of the Interior Bruce Babbitt, the National Parks and Conservation Association, and other opponents characterized it as a park closure bill aimed at dismantling the System. Sensitive to such charges, the House decisively defeated the bill in September 1995.

There was general agreement, however, that the procedures for identifying, studying, and recommending potential System additions needed reform. In November 1998 Congress again amended Section 8 of the General Authorities Act to require the Secretary to submit annually a list of areas recommended for study, based on established criteria of national significance, suitability, and feasibility. A new area study could not be made without specific congressional authorization. The Secretary was also directed to submit annual lists of primarily natural and primarily historical areas that had already been studied, in priority order for addition to the System. These requirements, it was hoped, would inhibit the promotion of unqualified park candidates.

The official categorization of each National Park System unit as natural, historical, or recreational beginning in 1964 was causing problems by the mid-1970s. This practice inadequately recognized the diversity of many if not most parks. Nearly all contained historic or cultural resources of at least local significance. The labeling of predominantly natural areas as recreational just because they permitted hunting or other uses disallowed by NPS policies for natural areas posed the greatest difficulty. Recreational area classification implied that natural preservation would be secondary to development for heavy public use—development and use that might be ecologically harmful. Environmentalists were especially disturbed about the recreational classification of such outstanding areas as Cape Cod National Seashore and Pictured Rocks National Lakeshore.

The NPS responded in 1975 by replacing its separate natural, historical, and recreational area policy manuals with a single management policy compilation addressing the range of characteristics each park possessed. A mostly natural area, for example, might also have important cultural features and portions suitable for recreational development. It would be zoned accordingly in its general management plan, and the various zones would be managed under policies tailored to each.

With this advance in planning and management sophistication, the assignment of each park to a single management category was no longer appropriate, and in 1977 Director Whalen officially abolished the area categories. For convenience, of course, most areas may still be identified informally as natural, historical, or recreational based on their primary attributes, as is done here.

Natural Areas

Thirty-seven predominantly natural areas in the present System were added, in whole or large part, from 1973 through 2004. Roughly half of them were in Alaska. Five new national parks outside Alaska incorporated previous national monuments: Biscayne, Florida; Channel Islands, Death Valley, and Joshua Tree, California; and Great Basin, Nevada. (Several other preexisting units were redesignated national parks without sufficient expansion to count them as additions.) The other areas outside Alaska were entirely new.

The first two of these, both authorized October 11, 1974, formed a new subcategory as well: Congress designated Big Cypress, Florida, and Big Thicket, Texas, as national preserves. The NPS explained national preserves as "primarily for the protection of certain resources. Activities such as hunting and fishing or the extraction of minerals and fuels may be permitted if they do not jeopardize the natural values." Although such uses had rendered other areas ineligible for natural classification and had caused them to be labeled recreational, Big Cypress and Big Thicket were even less suited for the latter category. The two preserves intensified the awkwardness of the management categories and became another argument for their abandonment in 1977.

Big Cypress National Preserve, encompassing 716,000 acres adjoining Everglades National Park on the northwest, was established primarily to protect the freshwater supply essential to the Everglades ecosystem. Containing abundant tropical plant and animal life, it continues to serve the Miccosukee and Seminole Indian tribes for subsistence hunting, fishing, and trapping and traditional ceremonies. Big Thicket National Preserve includes a significant portion of the Big Thicket area of East Texas. Its 96,680 acres protect dense growths of diverse plant species of great botanical interest at the crossroads of several North American plant and animal habitats.

John Day Fossil Beds, Oregon, and Hagerman Fossil Beds, Idaho, became national monuments by acts of Congress in 1974 and 1988. They joined Agate Fossil Beds, Dinosaur, Florissant Fossil Beds, and Fossil Butte national monuments among the System's important paleontological areas.

Congaree Swamp National Monument, South Carolina, authorized in 1976 and redesignated Congaree National Park in 2003, contains the last significant tract of virgin bottomland hardwoods in the Southeast. El Malpais National Monument, New Mexico, established in 1987, protects a volcanic landscape. Among other 1988 additions were Timucuan Ecological and Historic Preserve, a diverse salt marsh area in northeastern Florida; the National Park of American Samoa, containing tropical rain forests, beaches, and coral reefs; and City of Rocks National Reserve, a landscape of historical as well as geological interest in southern Idaho. Following the 1978 prototype of Ebey's Landing National Historical Reserve in Washington, City of Rocks's designation denoted an arrangement whereby the administration of acquired lands would be transferred to state or local governments once they had established zoning or other land protection measures in accord with a comprehensive plan.

The 1990s saw the addition of three all-new natural areas, although a good case could be made for assigning each to another category. Little River Canyon National Preserve, Alabama, containing a variety of rock formations, accommodates such recreational pursuits as kayaking, rock climbing, hunting, fishing, and trapping. Mojave National Preserve, California, covers 1,450,000 acres of the Mojave Desert also subject to diverse recreational activities. And Tallgrass Prairie National Preserve, Kansas, mostly owned by the National Park Trust, includes a historic ranch complex along with a prime remnant of the once vast tallgrass prairie ecosystem.

Great Sand Dunes National Preserve, created in 2000, encompasses 42,000 acres adjacent to Great Sand Dunes National Park. Virgin Islands Coral Reef National Monument was established in 2001 to protect the coral reef life, sandy beaches, and forests, and to preserve the rich cultural history of the region. Craters of the Moon National Preserve in Idaho was created in 2002 from 410,000 acres that had been added to Craters of the Moon National Monument. The preserve includes lava fields and sagebrush steppe grasslands.

Historical Areas
Seventy-eight additions from 1973 through 2004, more than half the period's total, deal primarily with American history. Twenty of these are military and Presidential sites. The great majority address themes that formerly received less attention in the System.

The bicentennial of the American Revolution was a major focus of National Park Service activity in the mid-1970s, and three of the new parks contributed to that observance. Boston National Historical Park, a mosaic of properties in public and private ownership, includes the Bunker Hill Monument, Dorchester Heights, Faneuil Hall, Old North Church, Old South Meeting House, and the Charlestown Navy Yard—berth for the USS *Constitution*. Valley Forge, long a Pennsylvania state park, became a national historical park on the bicentennial date of July 4, 1976. Ninety Six National Historic Site, South Carolina, authorized the next month, was the scene of military action in 1781.

Lewis and Clark National Historical Park (which incorporated Fort Clatsop National Memorial) was established in 2004 during the bicentennial of Lewis and Clark's expedition. Congress authorized Palo Alto Battlefield National Historic Site, Texas, to recognize the first important Mexican War battle on American soil. Cedar Creek and Belle Grove National Historical Park was established in 2002 to preserve a major Civil War battlefield and plantation in Virginia's Shenandoah Valley. Governors Island National Monument in New York, proclaimed in 2001, preserves the military defenses Castle Williams and Fort Jay, which date from before the War of 1812.

The USS *Arizona* Memorial at Pearl Harbor, Hawaii, and War in the Pacific National Historical Park on Guam commemorate important military events of World War II, while Manzanar National Historic Site, California, and Minidoka Internment National Monument, Idaho, interpret the wartime internment of Japanese Americans. Rosie the Riveter/World War II Home Front National Historical Park in California commemorates the contributions of those who supported the war effort. The World War II Memorial and the Korean War Veterans Memorial in Washington, D.C., honor those who fought and died in those wars. The Vietnam Veterans Memorial, also in Washington, bears the names of more than 58,000 dead and missing in Vietnam. Minuteman Missile National Historic Site, preserves remnants of a Cold War ICBM installation in South Dakota.

Two sites of terrorist attacks joined the National Park System during this period. The Oklahoma City National Memorial (established in 1997; abolished 2004) commemorates those affected by the 1995 bombing of the Alfred P. Murrah Federal Building in Oklahoma City. Flight 93 National Memorial in Pennsylvania honors the passengers and crew who sacrificed their lives to thwart a planned attack on the Nation's Capital on September 11, 2001. The Presidential sites include a landscaped memorial to Lyndon B. Johnson in Washington, D.C., and residences of Martin Van Buren in Kinderhook, New York; Ulysses S. Grant in St. Louis County, Missouri; James A. Garfield in Mentor, Ohio; Harry S Truman in Independence, Missouri; and Jimmy Carter in Plains, Georgia. Although Congress had authorized the Franklin Delano Roosevelt Memorial in Washington, D.C., in 1959, it was not completed and dedicated until 1997.

The arts and literature made significant progress in the System with the addition of parks for playwright Eugene O'Neill near Danville, California; author and critic Edgar Allan Poe in Philadelphia; landscape architect and author Frederick Law Olmsted in Brookline,

Bunker Hill Monument and statue of Col. William Prescott at Boston National Historical Park.

Massachusetts; impressionist painter J. Alden Weir in Ridgefield, Connecticut; and pioneer conservationist George Perkins Marsh, author of *Man and Nature* (1864), in Woodstock, Vermont. Congress authorized Dayton Aviation Heritage National Historical Park, Ohio, to further commemorate the Wright Brothers but also to recognize the African American poet Paul Laurence Dunbar at his Dayton house. New Orleans Jazz National Historical Park was intended to interpret the evolution of jazz in that city.

Among new parks treating social and humanitarian movements, five focus on women: Clara Barton National Historic Site, containing the Glen Echo, Maryland, house of the founder of the American Red Cross; Eleanor Roosevelt National Historic Site, preserving her retreat at Hyde Park, New York; Women's Rights National Historical Park, including Elizabeth Cady Stanton's house and other sites related to the early women's rights movement in Seneca Falls, New York; and Mary McLeod Bethune Council House National Historic Site in Washington, D.C., former headquarters of an organization Bethune established to improve the lives of black women. First Ladies National Historic Site in Ohio focuses on the lives and contributions of First Ladies and other notable women in American history.

The System paid African American history more attention at eight additions beyond the Dayton, New Orleans Jazz, and Bethune areas. Tuskegee Institute National Historic Site, Alabama, includes portions of the pioneering industrial education school established by Booker T. Washington in 1881. The nearby Tuskegee Airmen National Historic Site was a training ground for black Army Air Corps pilots in World War II. Maggie L. Walker National Historic Site, Virginia, contains the house of a leading figure in Richmond's black community during the early 20th century.

Boston African American National Historic Site comprises an antebellum meetinghouse and more than a dozen other historic structures. Martin Luther King, Jr., National Historic Site includes the Atlanta birthplace, church, and tomb of the civil rights leader. Brown v. Board of Education National Historic Site contains the segregated school in Topeka, Kansas, attended by Linda Brown, a plaintiff in the case leading to the 1954 U.S. Supreme Court decision outlawing legal racial segregation in public schools. Little Rock Central High School National Historic Site, Arkansas, commemorates that school's significant role in implementing the desegregation decision. Nicodemus National Historic Site includes remnants of a western Kansas town established by black emigrants from the South in the 1870s.

There were two additions in the nation's capital beyond those already mentioned. Constitution Gardens covers a part of Potomac

Park occupied until 1970 by "temporary" World War I military office buildings; its centerpiece is a memorial to the signers of the Declaration of Independence. Pennsylvania Avenue National Historic Site had been designated by Secretary Udall in 1965 to support the avenue's redevelopment, a tactic recalling the Jefferson National Expansion Memorial designation in St. Louis 30 years before. In the case of Pennsylvania Avenue, however, the plans were revised in the 1970s to provide for much historic preservation. The NPS assumed increasing management responsibilities along the avenue as it was redeveloped, justifying the site's listing as a System unit in 1987.

Five additions other than Dayton Aviation Heritage deal with America's industrial, commercial, and transportation history. Springfield Armory, Massachusetts, made a national historic site in 1974, was a center for the manufacture of military small arms and the scene of many technological advances from 1794 to 1968. Lowell National Historical Park, also in Massachusetts, includes 19th-century factories, a power canal system, and other elements of the nation's first planned industrial community.

Established in 1978, the park helped revitalize Lowell's depressed economy and inspired several other communities to seek similar assistance during the next decades. One was Scranton, Pennsylvania, where Congress authorized Steamtown National Historic Site in 1986. Steamtown was among the most controversial additions of the period; its primary resource was not a site but an eclectic collection of railroad locomotives and cars whose national significance was questioned by railroad historians. Furthermore, it was created through an appropriations act rather than by traditional legislative means, and the high cost of needed restoration promised to make it among the most expensive historical areas in the System. Keweenaw National Historical Park in Michigan's Upper Peninsula, established in 1992, preserves features associated with the first significant copper mining in the United States. New Bedford Whaling National Historical Park, Massachusetts, authorized in 1996, includes the New Bedford Whaling Museum and other properties illustrating the city's preeminent role in the whaling industry and recognizing its links to Native Alaskan whaling.

Most of the cultural properties assigned to the NPS upon its creation in 1916 dealt with American Indians, and such properties continued as a major component of the National Park System throughout its evolution. Outside Alaska there were four entirely new parks in this category from 1973 through 2004.

Knife River Indian Villages National Historic Site, North Dakota, contains important Hidatsa village remnants. Kaloko-Honokōhau National Historical Park includes fishponds, fish traps, village sites, and other archeological evidences of Hawaiian native culture. Poverty Point National Monument in northeastern Louisiana preserves traces of a culture that flourished during the first and second millennia B.C.E. Petroglyph National Monument, New Mexico, displays rock inscriptions of both prehistoric and more recent origin and has contemporary cultural significance.

Four previous national monuments treating American Indians and Spanish missions in the Southwest and one in Ohio dealing with an earlier civilization were incorporated in expanded parks. Chaco Culture National Historical Park superseded Chaco Canyon National Monument and added 33 outlying "Chaco Culture Archeological Protection Sites" for which Congress authorized special protective measures. Salinas Pueblo Missions National Monument incorporated the old Gran Quivira National Monument and two New Mexico state monuments containing Pueblo Indian and Spanish mission remains. Tumacacori National Historical Park encompassed the mission at the former Tumacacori National Monument and two nearby mission sites. Pecos National Historical Park combined the pueblo and mission at its predecessor monument with sites of the Civil War battle of Glorieta Pass, where Union troops blocked a Confederate attempt to take the Southwest in 1862. In Ohio, Mound City Group National Monument was supplanted by Hopewell Culture National Historical Park, containing additional earthworks left by those living here between 200 B.C.E. and 500 C.E.

Recreational Areas

Twenty areas that would have once been categorized as recreational joined the System in the 1973–2004 period. One was a national seashore, one was a reservoir-based area, four were urban recreation areas, two were national scenic trails, and the remainder were river areas of various designations.

Canaveral National Seashore, authorized in 1975, is the most recent national seashore. It occupies 25 miles of an undeveloped barrier island on Florida's Atlantic coast supporting many species of birds and other wildlife. The lands and waters administered by the NPS adjoin the Kennedy Space Center and Merritt Island National Wildlife Refuge. Emphasizing natural preservation, Canaveral's legislation prohibits new development beyond that necessary for public safety and proper administration.

Chickasaw National Recreation Area, Oklahoma, the reservoir addition, supplanted Arbuckle National Recreation Area and Platt National Park in 1976. Because Platt had never measured up to its prestigious designation, incorporation of the small mineral spring park in the national recreation area was a welcome solution to an old problem. Congress established Cuyahoga Valley National Recreation Area, between Cleveland and Akron, Ohio, to preserve "the historic, scenic, natural, and recreational values of the Cuyahoga River and the adjacent lands of the Cuyahoga Valley" and to maintain "needed recreational open space necessary to the urban environment." Its 32,525 acres include part of the Ohio and Erie Canal previously designated a national historic landmark. In 2000 it was redesignated Cuyahoga Valley National Park. Although considerably smaller, Chattahoochee River National Recreation Area outside Atlanta was designed to serve similar purposes for that metropolitan area.

Santa Monica Mountains National Recreation Area was authorized on 150,000 acres of rugged chapparal-covered landscape fronting on the beaches northwest of Los Angeles. Congress prescribed its management "in a manner which will preserve and enhance its scenic, natural, and historical setting and its public health value as an airshed for the Southern California metropolitan area while providing for the recreational and educational needs of the visiting public." Boston Harbor Islands National Recreation Area, comprising 30 islands, was to be managed in a partnership with state and local governments and other organizations; all but five of its 1,482 acres would remain in nonfederal ownership.

Congress authorized Natchez Trace National Scenic Trail, paralleling the Natchez Trace Parkway, and Potomac Heritage National Scenic Trail, from the mouth of the Potomac to its Pennsylvania headwaters, together in 1983. The NPS selected four segments of the former totaling 110 miles near Natchez and Jackson, Mississippi, and Nashville, Tennessee, for development as hiking and horseback trails. Of the latter's projected 704 miles, 271 miles comprising the existing Mount Vernon bicycle path, C&O Canal towpath, and Laurel Highlands Trail in Pennsylvania had been designated by 1999.

The first national river of the period added to the System was Big South Fork National River and Recreation Area, centered on the Big South Fork of the Cumberland River and its tributaries in Tennessee and Kentucky. The area's scenic gorges and valleys encompass numerous natural and historic features. Next came Obed Wild and Scenic River in East Tennessee, where the Obed and its principal tributaries cut through the Cumberland Plateau. The National Parks and Recreation Act of 1978 authorized five river additions: Middle Delaware National Scenic River, the portion of the Delaware within Delaware Water Gap National Recreation Area; Upper Delaware Scenic and Recreational River, including most of the Delaware between Pennsylvania and New York; Missouri National Recreational River, one of the last free-flowing stretches of the Missouri between Nebraska and South Dakota; New River Gorge National River, West Virginia, encompassing a rugged section of one of the oldest rivers on the continent; and Rio Grande Wild and Scenic River, including 191 miles of the American bank of the Rio Grande downstream from Big Bend National Park, Texas.

Congress authorized the next three river areas a decade later, in 1988. Mississippi National River and Recreation Area encompasses 69 miles of the Mississippi between Dayton and Hastings, Minnesota. Bluestone National Scenic River in southwestern West Virginia offers fishing, boating, and hiking as well as scenery; Gauley River National Recreation Area, also in West Virginia, presents one of the most exciting whitewater boating opportunities in the East. The most recent river additions followed in 1991 and 1992: Niobrara National Scenic River, Nebraska, and Great Egg Harbor Scenic and Recreational River, New Jersey.

Additions in Alaska

Climaxing one of the 20th century's great conservation campaigns, vast additions to the National Park System in Alaska in 1978–80 remain so significant as to warrant separate discussion.

Thanks to George Hartzog and others, the Alaska Native Claims Settlement Act of December 18, 1971, contained a provision of great consequence for land conservation. It directed the Secretary of the Interior to withdraw from selection by the state or native groups, or from disposition under the public land laws, up to 80 million acres that he deemed "suitable for addition to or creation as units of the National Park, Forest, Wildlife Refuge, and Wild and Scenic Rivers Systems." The Secretary had two years to make specific recommendations for additions to the four systems from the withdrawn lands. The recommended additions would remain withdrawn until Congress acted or for five years, whichever came first.

On the second anniversary deadline, Secretary Rogers Morton transmitted his recommendations. They included 32.3 million acres for parks, at a time when the existing System comprised some 31 million acres. The recommendations were controversial, especially in Alaska, where there was great opposition to so much land being removed from uses incompatible with park status. Bills introduced by supporters and opponents made little headway until the 95th Congress in 1977-78, the last years for legislative action before the withdrawals expired. A strong conservation bill then introduced by Rep. Morris K. Udall of Arizona incorporated the national preserve concept to allow for sport hunting in areas bearing that designation rather than in certain national parks, as Morton had proposed.

The House passed a modified version of Udall's bill in May 1978, but Alaska's senators blocked action on a comparable Senate bill, and the 95th Congress adjourned that October without an Alaska lands act. The land withdrawals would expire December 18. Faced with this prospect, President Jimmy Carter on December 1 took the extraordinary step of proclaiming 15 new national monuments and two major monument additions on the withdrawn lands. Two of the new monuments were under Forest Service jurisdiction and two under the Fish and Wildlife Service; the other 11 were additions to the National Park System. (The Fish and Wildlife Service monuments were subsequently incorporated in national wildlife refuges; the Forest Service monuments, Admiralty Island and Misty Fjords, retain their identities under that bureau.) The monuments were stopgaps, intended to withhold the areas from other disposition until Congress could reconsider and act on protective legislation.

Bills were reintroduced in the 96th Congress, and a revised bill sponsored by Udall and Rep. John Anderson of Illinois passed the House in May 1979. Alaska's senators, backed by a range of commercial interests and sportsmen's groups, again fought to limit additions to the restrictive national park and wildlife refuge systems. A somewhat weaker conservation bill finally cleared the Senate in August 1980. After President Carter's loss to Ronald Reagan that November, supporters of the House bill decided to accept the Senate's version rather than risk an impasse before adjournment and a less acceptable outcome in the next Congress. The House approved the Senate bill, and on December 2, 1980, Carter signed into law the Alaska National Interest Lands Conservation Act (ANILCA).

ANILCA gave the National Park System more than 47 million acres, exceeding the nearly 45 million acres assigned it by the provisional national monument proclamations and surpassing by nearly 50 percent the 32.3 million acres proposed seven years before. The act converted most of the national monuments to national parks and national preserves, the latter permitting sport hunting and trapping. As the 1950 act settling the Jackson Hole National Monument controversy had done in Wyoming, it also curtailed further expansion of the National Park System in Alaska by Presidential proclamation.

Before December 1978 Alaska had contained one national park, two national monuments, and two national historical parks. After December 1980 Alaska contained eight national parks, two national

Yentna Glacier with Mt. Russell icefall entering from left, Denali National Park, Alaska.

monuments, 10 national preserves, two national historical parks, and a wild river. Mount McKinley National Park was renamed Denali National Park after the Indian name for the mountain, which remained officially Mount McKinley, and was joined by a Denali National Preserve. The park and preserve together are more than four million acres larger than the old park. The old Glacier Bay and Katmai monuments became national parks, with adjoining national preserves. The Glacier Bay park and preserve gained some 478,000 acres over the old monument, while the two Katmai areas exceed the old Katmai monument by more than 1,300,000 acres.

Wrangell-St. Elias National Park contains 8,323,618 acres. Adjacent Wrangell-St. Elias National Preserve encompasses 4,852,773 acres. Together they are larger than the combined area of Vermont and New Hampshire and contain the continent's greatest array of glaciers and peaks above 16,000 feet—among them Mount St. Elias, rising second only to Mount McKinley in the United States. With Canada's adjacent Kluane National Park, this is one of the greatest parkland regions in the world. Gates of the Arctic National Park, all of whose 7,523,898 acres lie north of the Arctic Circle, and the 948,629-acre national preserve of the same name include part of the Central Brooks Range, the northernmost extension of the Rockies. Gentle valleys, wild rivers, and numerous lakes complement the jagged mountain peaks. Adjoining Gates of the Arctic on the west is Noatak National Preserve. Its 6,570,000 acres, drained by the Noatak River running through the 65-mile-long Grand Canyon of the Noatak, contain a striking array of plant and animal life and hundreds of archeological sites in what is the largest undeveloped river basin in the United States.

Kobuk Valley National Park, another Arctic area of 1,750,737 acres, adjoins the south border of Noatak National Preserve. Its diverse terrain includes the northernmost extent of the boreal forest and the 25-square-mile Great Kobuk Sand Dunes, the largest active dune field in arctic latitudes. Archeological remains are especially rich, revealing more than 10,000 years of human activity.

Cape Krusenstern National Monument, north of Kotzebue on the Chukchi Sea, was the single 1978–80 Alaska addition of predominantly cultural rather than natural significance. Embracing 650,000 acres, it is by far the largest such area in the System. One hundred fourteen lateral beach ridges formed by changing sea levels and wave action display chronological evidence of 5,000 years of marine mammal hunting by Inuit peoples. Older archeological sites are found inland. Bering Land Bridge National Preserve, with 2,698,000 acres on the Seward Peninsula, covers a remnant of the isthmus that connected

North America and Asia more than 13,000 years ago. Modern Inuit manage their reindeer herds in and around the preserve, which features rich paleontological and archeological resources, large migratory bird populations, ash explosion craters, and lava flows.

The 2,619,859-acre Lake Clark National Park and the 1,410,641-acre Lake Clark National Preserve are set in the heart of the Chigmit Mountains on the western shore of Cook Inlet, southwest of Anchorage. The 50-mile-long Lake Clark, largest of more than 20 glacial lakes, is fed by hundreds of waterfalls from the surrounding mountains and is headwaters for an important red salmon spawning ground. Jagged peaks and granite spires inspire the nickname "Alaskan Alps."

Yukon-Charley Rivers National Preserve protects 115 miles of the Yukon and the entire 88-mile Charley River basin within its 2,526,509 acres. Abandoned cabins and other cultural remnants recall the Yukon's role during the 1898 Gold Rush. The Charley, running swift and clear, is renowned for whitewater recreation. Grizzly bears, Dall sheep, and moose are among the abundant wildlife. Kenai Fjords National Park contains 670,643 acres. On the Gulf of Alaska near Seward, it is named for the scenic glacier-carved fjords along its coast. Above is the Harding Icefield, one of four major ice caps in the United States, from which radiate 34 major glacier arms. Sea lions and other marine mammals abound in the coastal waters.

The smallest of the new Alaska parks, preserves, and monuments is Aniakchak National Monument, whose 137,176 acres lie on the harsh Aleutian Peninsula south of Katmai. It is adjoined by the 465,603-acre Aniakchak National Preserve. Their central feature is the great Aniakchak Caldera, a 30-square-mile crater of a collapsed volcano. Within the caldera are a cone from later volcanic activity, lava flows, explosion pits, and Surprise Lake, which is heated by hot springs and cascades through a rift in the crater wall. ANILCA also designated 13 wild rivers for NPS administration. Twelve are entirely within parks, monuments, and preserves and are not listed as discrete NPS units. Part of the remaining one, Alagnak Wild River, lies outside and westward of Katmai, so it is counted separately. It offers salmon sport fishing and whitewater floating.

Overall the Alaska park additions are as superlative in quality as they are in quantitative terms. Although political and economic arguments were raised against them, there was little argument about the inherent natural and cultural merits that made the lands so clearly eligible for the National Park System. They have enriched it immeasurably.

1973	Dec. 28	Lyndon Baines Johnson Memorial Grove on the Potomac, District of Columbia
1974	March 7	Big South Fork NR and Recreation Area, Kentucky and Tennessee (assigned to NPS 1976)
	Aug. 1	Constitution Gardens, District of Columbia
	Oct. 1	Boston NHP, Massachusetts
	Oct. 11	Big Cypress N PRES, Florida
	Oct. 11	Big Thicket N PRES, Texas
	Oct. 26	Clara Barton NHS, Maryland
	Oct. 26	John Day Fossil Beds NM, Oregon
	Oct. 26	Knife River Indian Villages NHS, North Dakota
	Oct. 26	Martin Van Buren NHS, New York
	Oct. 26	Springfield Armory NHS, Massachusetts
	Oct. 26	Tuskegee Institute NHS, Alabama
	Dec. 27	Cuyahoga Valley NRA, Ohio (redesignated Cuyahoga Valley NP 2000)
1975	Jan. 3	Canaveral NS, Florida
1976	March 17	Chickasaw NRA, Oklahoma (incorporated Platt NP and Arbuckle NRA)
	June 30	Klondike Gold Rush NHP, Alaska and Washington
	July 4	Valley Forge NHP, Pennsylvania
	Aug. 19	Ninety Six NHS, South Carolina
	Oct. 12	Obed WSR, Tennessee
	Oct. 18	Congaree Swamp NM, South Carolina (redesignated Congaree NP 2003)
	Oct. 18	Eugene O'Neill NHS, California
	Oct. 21	Monocacy NB, Maryland (reauthorization and redesignation of Monocacy NMP)
1977	May 26	Eleanor Roosevelt NHS, New York
1978	June 5	Lowell NHP, Massachusetts
	Aug. 15	Chattahoochee NRA, Georgia
	Aug. 18	War in the Pacific NHP, Guam
	Oct. 19	Fort Scott NHS, Kansas
	Nov. 10	*National Parks and Recreation Act*
	Nov. 10	Ebey's Landing NH RES, Washington
	Nov. 10	Edgar Allan Poe NHS, Pennsylvania
	Nov. 10	Friendship Hill NHS, Pennsylvania
	Nov. 10	Jean Lafitte NHP & PRES, Louisiana (incorporated Chalmette NHP)
	Nov. 10	Kaloko-Honokōhau NHP, Hawaii
	Nov. 10	Maggie L. Walker NHS, Virginia
	Nov. 10	Middle Delaware NSR, Pennsylvania and New Jersey
	Nov. 10	Missouri National Recreational River, Nebraska and South Dakota
	Nov. 10	New River Gorge NR, West Virginia
	Nov. 10	Palo Alto Battlefield NHS, Texas

1978	Nov. 10	Rio Grande WSR, Texas
	Nov. 10	Saint Paul's Church NHS, New York (designated 1943)
	Nov. 10	San Antonio Missions NHP, Texas
	Nov. 10	Santa Monica Mountains NRA, California
	Nov. 10	Thomas Stone NHS, Maryland
	Nov. 10	Upper Delaware SRR, Pennsylvania and New York
	Dec. 1	Aniakchak NM, Alaska (incorporated in legislated Aniakchak NM and Aniakchak N PRES by ANILCA 1980)
	Dec. 1	Bering Land Bridge NM, Alaska (redesignated a N PRES by ANILCA 1980)
	Dec. 1	Cape Krusenstern NM, Alaska
	Dec. 1	Denali NM, Alaska (incorporated with Mount McKinley NP in Denali NP and Denali N PRES by ANILCA 1980)
	Dec. 1	Gates of the Arctic NM, Alaska (incorporated in Gates of the Arctic NP and Gates of the Arctic N PRES by ANILCA 1980)
	Dec. 1	Glacier Bay NM, Alaska (addition to existing NM; total incorporated in Glacier Bay NP and Glacier Bay N PRES by ANILCA 1980)
	Dec. 1	Katmai NM, Alaska (addition to existing NM; total incorporated in Katmai NP and Katmai N PRES by ANILCA 1980)
	Dec. 1	Kenai Fjords NM, Alaska (redesignated a NP by ANILCA 1980)
	Dec. 1	Kobuk Valley NM, Alaska (redesignated a NP by ANILCA 1980)
	Dec. 1	Lake Clark NM, Alaska (incorporated in Lake Clark NP and Lake Clark N PRES by ANILCA 1980)
	Dec. 1	Noatak NM, Alaska (incorporated in Noatak N PRES by ANILCA 1980)
	Dec. 1	Wrangell-St. Elias NM, Alaska (incorporated in Wrangell-St. Elias NP and Wrangell-St. Elias N PRES by ANILCA 1980)
	Dec. 1	Yukon-Charley NM, Alaska (redesignated Yukon-Charley Rivers N PRES by ANILCA 1980)
1979	Oct. 12	Frederick Law Olmsted NHS, Massachusetts
1980	March 5	Channel Islands NP, California (incorporated Channel Islands NM)
	June 28	Biscayne NP, Florida (incorporated Biscayne NM)
	July 1	Vietnam Veterans Memorial, District of Columbia (dedicated 1982)
	Sept. 9	USS *Arizona* Memorial, Hawaii
	Oct. 10	Boston African American NHS, Massachusetts
	Oct. 10	Martin Luther King, Jr., NHS, Georgia
	Dec. 2	*Alaska National Interest Lands Conservation Act (ANILCA)*
	Dec. 2	Alagnak WR, Alaska
	Dec. 19	Chaco Culture NHP, New Mexico (incorporated Chaco Canyon NM)
	Dec. 19	Salinas NM, New Mexico (incorporated Gran Quivira NM; redesignated Salinas Pueblo Missions NM 1988)
	Dec. 22	Kalaupapa NHP, Hawaii
	Dec. 28	James A. Garfield NHS, Ohio

1980	Dec. 28	Women's Rights NHP, New York
1983	March 28	Natchez Trace NST, Mississippi, Alabama, and Tennessee
	March 28	Potomac Heritage NST, District of Columbia, Maryland, Pennsylvania, and Virginia
	May 23	Harry S Truman NHS, Missouri (designated 1982)
1986	Oct. 21	Steamtown NHS, Pennsylvania
	Oct. 27	Great Basin NP, Nevada (incorporated Lehman Caves NM)
	Oct. 28	Korean War Veterans Memorial, District of Columbia (dedicated 1995)
1987	June 25	Pennsylvania Avenue NHS, District of Columbia (designated 1965)
	Dec. 23	Jimmy Carter NHS, Georgia
	Dec. 31	El Malpais NM, New Mexico
1988	Feb. 16	Timucuan Ecological and Historic Preserve, Florida
	June 27	San Francisco Maritime NHP, California (formerly part of Golden Gate NRA)
	Sept. 8	Charles Pinckney NHS, South Carolina
	Oct. 7	Natchez NHP, Mississippi
	Oct. 31	National Park of American Samoa, American Samoa
	Oct. 31	Poverty Point NM, Louisiana
	Nov. 18	City of Rocks N RES, Idaho
	Nov. 18	Hagerman Fossil Beds NM, Idaho
	Nov. 18	Mississippi NRRA, Minnesota
	Dec. 26	Bluestone NSR, West Virginia
	Dec. 26	Gauley River NRA, West Virginia
1989	Oct. 2	Ulysses S. Grant NHS, Missouri
1990	June 27	Pecos NHP, New Mexico (incorporated Pecos NM)
	June 27	Petroglyph NM, New Mexico
	Aug. 6	Tumacacori NHP, Arizona (incorporated Tumacacori NM)
	Oct. 31	Weir Farm NHS, Connecticut
1991	May 24	Niobrara NSR, Nebraska
	Dec. 11	Mary McLeod Bethune Council House NHS, District of Columbia (designated 1982)
1992	Feb. 24	Salt River Bay NHP and Ecological Preserve, Virgin Islands
	March 3	Manzanar NHS, California
	May 27	Hopewell Culture NHP, Ohio (incorporated Mound City Group NM)
	Aug. 26	Marsh-Billings NHP, Vermont (redesignated Marsh-Billings-Rockefeller NHP 1998)
	Oct. 16	Dayton Aviation Heritage NHP, Ohio
	Oct. 21	Little River Canyon N PRES, Alabama
	Oct. 26	Brown v. Board of Education NHS, Kansas
	Oct. 27	Great Egg Harbor SRR, New Jersey

1992	Oct. 27	Keweenaw NHP, Michigan
1994	Oct. 31	Death Valley NP, California and Nevada (incorporated Death Valley NM)
	Oct. 31	Joshua Tree NP, California (incorporated Joshua Tree NM)
	Oct. 31	Mojave N PRES, California
	Oct. 31	New Orleans Jazz NHP, Louisiana
	Nov. 2	Cane River Creole NHP, Louisiana
1996	Nov. 12	Boston Harbor Islands NRA, Massachusetts
	Nov. 12	New Bedford Whaling NHP, Massachusetts
	Nov. 12	Nicodemus NHS, Kansas
	Nov. 12	Tallgrass Prairie N PRES, Kansas
	Nov. 12	Washita Battlefield NHS, Oklahoma
1997	Oct. 9	Oklahoma City N MEM, Oklahoma (abolished 2004)
1998	Nov. 6	Little Rock Central High School NHS, Arkansas
	Nov. 6	Tuskegee Airmen NHS, Alabama
1999	Nov. 29	Minuteman Missile NHS, South Dakota
2000	Oct. 11	First Ladies NHS, Ohio
	Oct. 24	Rosie the Riveter/World War II Home Front NHP, California
	Nov. 22	Great Sand Dunes N PRES, Colorado
2001	Jan. 17	Virgin Islands Coral Reef NM, Virgin Islands
	Jan. 17	Minidoka Internment NM, Idaho
	Jan. 20	Governors Island NM, New York
2002	Aug. 27	Craters of the Moon N PRES, Idaho
	Sept. 24	Flight 93 N MEM, Pennsylvania
	Dec. 19	Cedar Creek and Belle Grove NHP, Virginia
2004	May 29	World War II Memorial, District of Columbia
	Sept. 30	Lewis and Clark NHP, Oregon and Washington (incorporated Fort Clatsop N MEM)

IHS   International Historic Site
NB   National Battlefield
NBP   National Battlefield Park
NBS   National Battlefield Site
NHP   National Historical Park
NHP & PRES   National Historical Park and Preserve
NH RES   National Historical Reserve
NHS   National Historic Site
NL   National Lakeshore

NM   National Monument
NM & PRES   National Monument and Preserve
N MEM   National Memorial
NMP   National Military Park
NP   National Park
NP & PRES   National Park and Preserve
N PRES   National Preserve
NR   National River
NRA   National Recreation Area

NRRA   National River and Recreation Area
N RES   National Reserve
NS   National Seashore
NSR   National Scenic River/Riverway
NST   National Scenic Trail
PKWY   Parkway
SRR   Scenic and Recreational River
WR   Wild River
WSR   Wild and Scenic River

Ideals Into Reality

All national parklands are not created equal. Besides the obvious physical distinctions among and within the basic types of areas in the National Park System—natural and cultural, urban and wilderness, battlefield and birthplace, arctic and tropical—there are qualitative differences as well.

From the beginning, the National Park Service has professed to acquire only the most outstanding lands and resources, with "national significance" as the primary criterion. "In studying new park projects, you should seek to find scenery of supreme and distinctive quality or some natural feature so extraordinary or unique as to be of national interest and importance," declared the policy letter Horace Albright wrote for Secretary Lane's signature in 1918. "The national park system as now constituted should not be lowered in standard, dignity, and prestige by the inclusion of areas which express in less than the highest terms the particular class or kind of exhibit which they represent."

At its second meeting in May 1936, the Advisory Board on National Parks, Historic Sites, Buildings, and Monuments addressed historical parks in a similar policy statement prepared by Verne E. Chatelain, the Service's chief historian. "The general criterion in selecting areas administered by the Department of the Interior through the National Park Service whether natural or historic, is that they shall be outstanding examples in their respective classes," it declared. "The number of Federal areas must be necessarily limited, and care should be exercised to prevent the accumulation of sites of lesser rank."

Guidelines for evaluating national significance have been developed and refined over the years. The current criteria appear in the Service's Management Policies. A natural park should be an outstanding or rare example of a geologic landform or biotic area, a place of exceptional ecological or geological diversity, a site with a concentrated population of rare plant or animal species or unusually abundant fossil deposits, or an outstandingly scenic area. Historical parks should be associated with persons, events, or themes of national importance; should encompass structures or features of great intrinsic or representational value; or should contain archeological resources of major scientific consequence. Integrity is vital for natural and historical areas: they must not be so altered, deteriorated, or otherwise impaired that their significance cannot readily be appreciated by the public. The criteria for recreational areas stress spaciousness, high resource quality, proximity to major population centers, and potential for attracting national as well as local and regional visitation.

A few of the early parks and monuments did not measure up to the ideals expressed in these policies and criteria. Platt and Sullys Hill national parks, established just after the turn of the century, have been mentioned previously in this regard. Verendrye National Monument, North Dakota, proclaimed in 1917, was found to have no historical connection with the French explorer alleged to have visited the site. Fossil Cycad National Monument, South Dakota, later disclosed few of the fossils for which it had been proclaimed in 1922. In 1956 Congress approved Verendrye's transfer to the state and Fossil Cycad's return to the public domain. More than a dozen National Park System units have lost that status following reappraisal of their significance. A few other places of questionable national significance have been admitted to the System and remain in its ranks. What accounts for these imperfections?

In truth the professional guidelines for evaluating national significance have not always been foremost in the minds of those responsible for new parklands. The NPS customarily transmits its recommendations on new area legislation through the Interior Department to Congress, but Congress makes the final decisions. As a representative body, it normally and naturally will give greater weight to vocal public sentiment behind a park proposal than to abstract standards that might support a negative vote on it. A park bill backed by an influential constituency and lacking significant outside opposition is thus apt to proceed without great regard for the opinions of historians, scientists, or other professional specialists in the bureaucracy. Once established via this process, a park is unlikely to be abolished or removed to other custody.

Can Congress be blamed for the System's shortcomings, then? Not entirely. The NPS itself is no ivory tower institution, immune from

The Liberty Bell, shown here in 1954, draws visitors from all over the world to Independence National Historical Park, Philadelphia, Pennsylvania.

public and political pressures. It is a government bureau dependent on congressional appropriations and popular support for its survival and prosperity. From its earliest days, Stephen Mather, Horace Albright, and most of their successors sought to enlarge its public and political constituencies by acquiring more parks in more places: natural areas in the East, the military parks and other historic sites, parkways, reservoir areas, seashores, urban recreation areas. These aims have made most NPS managers reluctant to vigorously resist popular park proposals questioned mostly by their professional advisers; they have seen little advantage in opposing the desires of influential members of Congress for parks in their districts. Under the circumstances it is hardly surprising that all parks do not equal the System's so-called "crown jewels."

The System has also been faulted for its unevenness in representing America's natural and cultural heritage. The idea that there should be parks for all the major facets of natural and human history underlay the 1972 *National Park System Plan*. As the expansionist impulse behind that document cooled in the next decade, its rationale came under critical scrutiny. Extant sites and related physical features capable of being preserved and appreciated by park visitors are not evenly dispersed among the many themes of human history, nor are all themes well communicated via such resources. The fact that the System deals more with military history than the history of philosophy or education, for example, may be justified by the nature and availability of sites and structures, the System's primary historical media.

Most natural geographic features or phenomena are able to be represented by parks, but judging them all worthy of park representation oversteps the traditional concept of parks as places for public enjoyment. In *America's National Parks and Their Keepers* (Resources for the Future, 1984), Ronald A. Foresta faulted the natural history component of the *National Park System Plan* for relying on purely scientific criteria and ignoring the scenic or human appeal factor. "This comes close to abandoning the idea of a park altogether," he observed. "Perhaps some representative of exposed Silurian rock face should be preserved on a federally owned site. . . . There is no reason for such a site to be called a park, however, or for it to be part of the National Park System unless it has more to recommend it than pure representativeness."

At bottom, much of the controversy over what should be added to the System over the years has stemmed from different perceptions of what the System should be. Purists in and outside the NPS deplored the acquisition of such natural parks as Shenandoah, which had been cut over and existed in a less-than-primeval state. They and others who equated the System with natural preservation saw the influx of historical areas in the 1930s as diffusing its identity. Both natural and historical park partisans did not all welcome the parkways, the reservoir-based areas, and others added less for intrinsic resource quality than for recreational use. Some of these additions, typified by Gateway and Golden Gate, tended to be disproportionately demanding of funds and personnel—another reason for critics to begrudge them.

Today's System is both more and less than it might be. That it has edged into certain areas of essentially state and local concern was perhaps inevitable, evolving as it did over decades when the Federal Government enlarged its role in virtually every sphere. That its quality has sometimes been compromised was surely inevitable, given the public and political involvement in its evolution befitting a democratic society. That it incompletely and unevenly represents the nation's cultural and natural heritage has much to do with the physical nature and recreational—in the broad sense—purpose of parks.

All things considered, the wonder is not that the System has fallen short of the ideals set for it, but that it has come so close to them. In it are a remarkable array of the nation's greatest natural and historic places and recreational areas of outstanding attraction. Not every park is a Yellowstone, not every historic site boasts an Independence Hall. But nearly all have resources and values that make them something special—even nationally significant. With good reason the National Park System is among America's proudest and best-loved creations.

Part 3

Visitors at Crater Lake National Park, Oregon, 1938.

Two national park areas in the lower 48 states have adjoining national preserves that are separate units of the National Park System but managed jointly. They are Great Sand Dunes and Craters of the Moon.

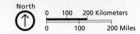

North

| 0 | 100 | 200 Kilometers |
| 0 | 100 | 200 Miles |

Noatak

Cape Krusenstern

Bering Land Bridge

Kobuk Valley

Gates of the Arctic

ALASKA

Yukon-Charley Rivers

Denali

Wrangell-St. Elias

Lake Clark

Alagnak

Kenai Fjords

Katmai

Klondike Gold Rush

Glacier Bay

Aniakchak

Sitka

Seven national park areas in Alaska have adjoining national preserves that are separate units of the National Park System but managed jointly. They are Aniakchak, Denali, Gates of the Arctic, Glacier Bay, Katmai, Lake Clark, and Wrangell-St. Elias.

HAWAII

USS *Arizona* Memorial

Kalaupapa

Haleakalā

Pu'ukoholā Heiau

Kaloko-Honokōhau

Pu'uhonua o Hōnaunau

Hawai'i Volcanoes

United States Territories

| AMERICAN SAMOA | GUAM | PUERTO RICO | VIRGIN ISLANDS |

National Park of American Samoa

War in the Pacific

San Juan

Salt River Bay

Virgin Islands
Virgin Islands Coral Reef
Buck Island Reef
Christiansted

As of December 31, 2004, the National Park System comprised 388 separate park areas in the United States and territories. These areas include national parks, national monuments, national battlefields, national historic sites, national recreation areas, national preserves, and a number of other designations. Complete lists of designations are shown below the charts at the end of the chapters.

All 388 park areas are shown on the maps on pages 110–112. The maps below and on pages 114–115 document the System's growth over time. They correspond chronologically with the chapters in this book; the additions from 1973 through 2004 appear on the last two maps, "1973–1990" and "1991–2004."

Shown in red on each map are the new additions for its time period.

Parks Authorized Before August 25, 1916

Alaska

Hawaii

United States Territories
American Samoa   Guam   Puerto Rico and the Virgin Islands

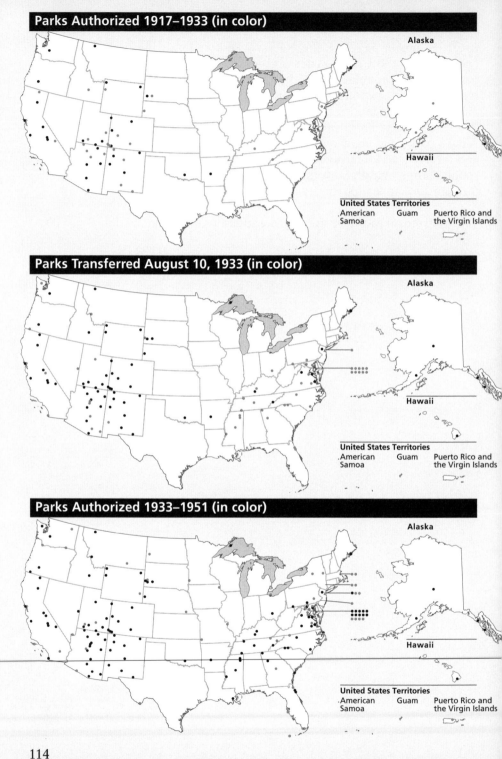

Parks Authorized 1917–1933 (in color)

Alaska

Hawaii

United States Territories
American   Guam   Puerto Rico and
Samoa   the Virgin Islands

Parks Transferred August 10, 1933 (in color)

Alaska

Hawaii

United States Territories
American   Guam   Puerto Rico and
Samoa   the Virgin Islands

Parks Authorized 1933–1951 (in color)

Alaska

Hawaii

United States Territories
American   Guam   Puerto Rico and
Samoa   the Virgin Islands

114

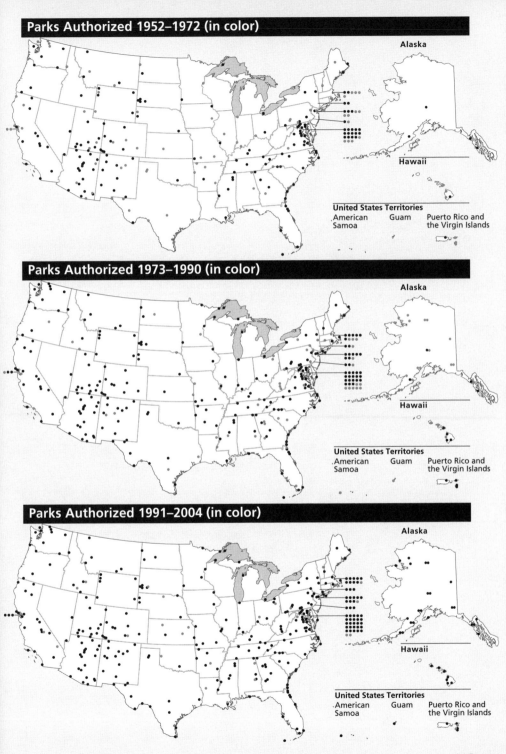

Parks Authorized 1952–1972 (in color)

Alaska

Hawaii

United States Territories

American Samoa   Guam   Puerto Rico and the Virgin Islands

Parks Authorized 1973–1990 (in color)

Alaska

Hawaii

United States Territories

American Samoa   Guam   Puerto Rico and the Virgin Islands

Parks Authorized 1991–2004 (in color)

Alaska

Hawaii

United States Territories

American Samoa   Guam   Puerto Rico and the Virgin Islands

115

Stephen T. Mather	May 16, 1917 - January 8, 1929
Horace M. Albright	January 12, 1929 - August 9, 1933
Arno B. Cammerer	August 10, 1933 - August 9, 1940
Newton B. Drury	August 20, 1940 - March 31, 1951
Arthur E. Demaray	April 1, 1951 - December 8, 1951
Conrad L. Wirth	December 9, 1951 - January 7, 1964
George B. Hartzog, Jr.	January 9, 1964 - December 31, 1972
Ronald H. Walker	January 7, 1973 - January 3, 1975
Gary Everhardt	January 13, 1975 - May 27, 1977
William J. Whalen	July 5, 1977 - May 13, 1980
Russell E. Dickenson	May 15, 1980 - March 3, 1985
William Penn Mott, Jr.	May 17, 1985 - April 16, 1989
James M. Ridenour	April 17, 1989 - January 20, 1993
Roger G. Kennedy	June 1, 1993 - March 29, 1997
Robert G. Stanton	August 4, 1997 - January 20, 2001
Fran P. Mainella	July 18, 2001 -

Horace M. Albright *(left)* and Stephen T. Mather, Los Angeles, California, 1928. Mather was the first director of the National Park Service; Albright was the second.

George Wright, ca. 1929

Freeman Tilden, 1969   Frederick Law Olmsted, ca. 1900

The national parks you visit today owe much to individuals who worked from both inside and outside the System to shape its landscape and philosophy. Among these were Frederick Law Olmsted, George Wright, and Freeman Tilden.

Frederick Law Olmsted (1822–1903) is the acknowledged father of landscape architecture in the United States. Well known for his naturalistic design for New York City's Central Park and many other urban parks, Olmsted was instrumental in the setting aside of Yosemite Valley and the Mariposa sequoia grove as the nation's first natural reservation in 1864. Yosemite became a national park in 1890. Frederick Law Olmsted National Historic Site in Brookline, Massachusetts, honors his life and work.

Working as a naturalist in Yosemite National Park in the 1920s, George Melendez Wright became increasingly concerned about the impact of humans on wildlife. As the Service's first chief of its wildlife division, he instituted formal studies of wild species, evaluating threats and proposing solutions for endangered species. In 1936 Wright died in an automobile accident at age 32. His holistic view of park management—that parklands are inseparable from the world around them—lives on through the George Wright Society.

Born in 1883 near Boston, Massachusetts, Freeman Tilden was a prolific writer from a young age. In the 1940s, at the urging of NPS director Newton Drury, Tilden began to write about national parks and their value to America's heritage. His focus soon shifted to the presentation of a park's story to visitors; he advocated not just a recitation of facts but the forging of a connection between the visitor and the park. Tilden's 1957 book *Interpreting Our Heritage* sets forth the guiding principles for how the National Park Service shapes the visitors' experience. Tilden died in 1980.

Suggested Readings

Albright, Horace M., and Robert Cahn. *The Birth of the National Park Service: The Founding Years, 1913-33*. Salt Lake City: Howe Brothers, 1985.

Albright, Horace M., and Marian Albright Schenck. *Creating the National Park Service: The Missing Years*. Norman: University of Oklahoma Press, 1999.

Butler, Mary Ellen. *Prophet of the Parks: The Story of William Penn Mott, Jr.* Ashburn, Virginia: National Recreation and Park Association, 1999.

Dilsaver, Lary M., ed. *America's National Park System: The Critical Documents*. Lanham, Maryland: Rowman & Littlefield, 1994.

Everhart, William C. *The National Park Service*. Boulder, Colorado: Westview Press, 1983.

Foresta, Ronald A. *America's National Parks and Their Keepers*. Washington, D.C.: Resources for the Future, 1985.

Hartzog, George B., Jr. *Battling for the National Parks*. Mt. Kisco, New York: Moyer Bell, 1988.

Ise, John. *Our National Park Policy: A Critical History*. Baltimore: Johns Hopkins Press, 1961.

Kaufman, Polly Welts. *National Parks and the Woman's Voice: A History*. Albuquerque: University of New Mexico Press, 1998.

Rettie, Dwight F. *Our National Park System: Caring for America's Greatest Natural and Historic Treasures*. Urbana: University of Illinois Press, 1995.

Ridenour, James M. *The National Parks Compromised: Pork Barrel Politics and America's Treasures*. Merrillville, Indiana: ICS Books, 1994.

Rothman, Hal K. *America's National Monuments: The Politics of Preservation*. Lawrence: University Press of Kansas, 1994.

Runte, Alfred. *National Parks: The American Experience*. 3d ed. Lincoln: University of Nebraska Press, 1997.

Sellars, Richard West. *Preserving Nature in the National Parks: A History*. New Haven: Yale University Press, 1997.

Shankland, Robert. *Steve Mather of the National Parks*. 3d ed. New York: Alfred A. Knopf, 1976.

Swain, Donald C. *Wilderness Defender: Horace M. Albright and Conservation*. Chicago: University of Chicago Press, 1970.

Wirth, Conrad L. *Parks, Politics, and the People*. Norman: University of Oklahoma Press, 1980.

Decals on the windshield of this car in 1922 reveal a love of travel through the American West.

All photos and illustrations used are from the National Park Service archives.

National Park Service

The mission of the Department of the Interior is to protect and provide access to our nation's natural and cultural heritage and to honor our trust responsibilities to tribes. The National Park Service preserves this heritage unimpaired in the National Park System for the enjoyment, education, and inspiration of this and future generations. The National Park Service cooperates with partners to extend the benefits of conservation and outdoor recreation throughout this country and the world. To learn more about national parks and National Park Service programs in America's communities, visit www.nps.gov.